52 Gospel-Centered Service Projects
for Families with Children of All Ages

Growing
—a—
Servant's
Heart

Jennifer Ohaneson

To
my friends who encouraged,
my children who sacrificed,
my Husband who believed,
and my Heavenly Father who led.
Thank you!

Contents

Letting Go of Expectations

Let's start with a reality check. Doing a service project every week for an entire year can be overwhelming. Let's be honest — most families are not going to do one project each week. You can let go of that expectation. I want you to use this book in a way that fits in with the unique needs and pace of your family. This means you can complete the service projects in one year — or over several years.

Some families already have a full plate of things to do, and they feel it would be too hard to add another activity to the schedule. However, as most parents already know, just because something is hard, doesn't mean it shouldn't be done. As you work through this book as a family, you will likely notice your children beginning to look forward to serving and even developing a desire to serve others.

As you complete the various service projects outlined in this book, you might find that some projects turn out differently than you expected. That's okay! The projects do not have to turn out perfectly. The focus should be glorifying God by doing each project with a servant's heart, while instilling Christ-honoring values into your children. Through these service projects, you are teaching your children practical ways to demonstrate the love of Christ to others, while also equipping them to live this way all the days of their lives.

The Purpose of This Book

Many years ago, I found myself struggling to find age-appropriate service projects to do with all my children. At the time, my children ranged in age from 2 years old to 16 years old. Given no options were available to serve with our entire family, I decided to give up my birthday one year to make care packages for a homeless shelter in Washington, DC. Little did I know that this service project would lead me to become the co-founder of a nonprofit ministry called Blessing Bags International. This ministry provides opportunities for my family and many other families with children of all ages to serve together. I never dreamed that the Lord would use this ministry to place a desire in me to provide more tools for families to easily serve together with their children regardless of age or physical abilities. Writing this book is one of the ways that I am continuing to obey the Lord.

Every Christian parent wants their children to one day make their faith their own — not to just mimic their family and follow their traditions. We long for our children to truly love the Lord. My desire in writing this book is to provide a tangible way to help parents raise a generation that both knows the Lord and the things he has done (Judges 2:10) by helping them to be doers of the word, not hearers only (James 1:22-25).

This book will provide age-appropriate opportunities to serve others, regardless of your child's age. You will find a variety of service projects covering a multitude of topics. I hope that the

Lord would not only increase your children's desire for serving others, but also ignite a passion in them leading them towards their God-given design. God created all of us with a purpose, and I pray through this book that God will ignite some of those passions and purposes in your children.

This book is also intended to be used as a journal. As your family and children grow, it can be used to reminisce and even repeat your favorite projects. When you are doing the service projects, make notes, highlight, underline, and journal about your experiences. In addition to creating lasting memories, this book will more importantly help your children on this journey to grow a servant's heart.

You may be wondering, "When is the right age to start serving?" It is never too soon to look for opportunities to serve together with your children. They are never too young for you to begin sowing seeds, which helps develop a servant's heart in each of your children regardless of age. Toddlers, preschoolers, and even kindergarteners may seem too young to fully understand some projects. However, that is not a reason for waiting to instill these values. As they take part in these service activities, you are setting the stage for service to become a regular part of their lives. I truly believe that you are never too young to make a difference.

I want to share a story with you. It will sound familiar to some and new to others. In either case, it is a beautiful story, reminding us that each of us can make a difference, and there isn't an age requirement for showing empathy.

A young child was on a beach, surrounded by thousands of starfish that had been stranded in the sand by the low tide. As the child was tossing them into the ocean one at a time, an old man walked by and asked, "Why are you throwing the starfish into the ocean?" The child responded, "Since the sun's up and the tide's going out, they will die if I don't throw them back in the water." Laughing, the old man said, "But there are miles of beach filled with starfish. You aren't making any difference." After listening politely, the young girl bent down, picked up another starfish, threw it into the sea, and said to the old man, "I made a difference for that one."

I love that story! When the problem seems too big, it is encouraging to focus on what you can do, instead of focusing on what you can't do. Each of us can choose to do something to make a difference in the lives of others. The difference is often far greater than we know.

Teaching your children to serve others is a crucial part of biblical parenting. In fact, it is the example set for us by Jesus. In Matthew 20:28, the Bible says, "even as the Son of Man came not to be served but to serve, and to give his life as a ransom for many." As you point your children to Jesus, you are pointing them to the greatest example of love and service to others.

We want to teach our children to serve rather than be served. It is easy to think of ourselves because it comes naturally to all of us. Thinking of others will take a lot more practice. Stick with it and know that your efforts are making a lasting impact on your children and helping them see the world and other people with love and compassion.

Each service project is broken down into the following 6 sections:

Scripture
Everything we do should be grounded in and point others back to God's Word. Our desire to train our children to love and serve others is based on the Scriptures outlined in the Bible.

Deuteronomy 6:5-7 says, "You shall love the Lord your God with all your heart and with all your soul and with all your might. And these words that I command you today shall be on your heart. You shall teach them diligently to your children, and shall talk of them when you sit in your house, and when you walk by the way, and when you lie down, and when you rise."

Mark 12:30-31 says, "And you shall love the Lord your God with all your heart and with all your soul and with all your mind and with all your strength. The second is this: 'You shall love your neighbor as yourself.' There is no other commandment greater than these."

12

Share these verses with your children. You could use these verses for each service project as a memory verse for that week.

Psalm 119:11 says, "I have stored up your word in my heart, that I might not sin against you."

Let's Talk

Parents, read this section ahead of time. The information provided is intended to give you a better understanding of the goal of the service project. After reviewing the information, you can tailor the content to share with your children based on their age and maturity level. Feel free to share as little or as much as you are comfortable with each week to help your children have a better understanding of the service project's purpose.

Let's Prep

This section is designed to help you plan ahead and have everything you need to be successful. Even the best-planned service projects can backfire if proper preparations aren't made. Whenever possible, allow children to be a part of this process. The more involved your children are in the service project, the greater the impact will be on them.

Be sure to set realistic expectations for each service project. Take time to go over what is expected of your child and help them know their role. When you prepare ahead of time, the extra effort will help your service project run a lot more smoothly.

Let's Serve

This section walks you through how to get started with the fun stuff! Remember, get the whole family involved by giving everyone a task. Every age, from toddlers to teens, can make an impact! When children are given responsibility, they feel valued and rise to the occasion. As your children begin to realize the impact being made by serving others, you will truly begin to see how serving together is developing a servant's heart in them.

Don't miss out on such teachable moments. You might notice your children helping someone unload a grocery cart, holding a door for someone, or maybe even cleaning up messes without being asked. When your children naturally serve others, be sure not to discourage them. Rather, affirm and encourage your children when you see this behavior.

Help your children represent Jesus with excellence! Always point others and your children back to God and His love, which is our reason for serving. When possible, link service projects back to your church, instead of yourself. By doing this, you are teaching your children that we are not seeking approval of man but of God.

Let's Pray

In this section, a prayer is provided that relates to the service project. You could use this prayer or improvise with your own prayer based on your specific experience during the service project.

As we strive to grow a servant's hearts in our children, may we continue to pray for the people we serve, even after the project is complete. This will help remind your little ones that their service was not just to a person, but to the Lord.

If a project doesn't seem right for your family or if you're on a tight budget, don't just skip the project. Prayer can be done instead of any of the service projects in this book.

Let's Reflect

This section is provided for journaling your experience after each service project. As you talk to your children about your family's experience, be sure to ask questions and include all of your children. These discussions are a great time to revisit the reason why you were doing the service project. Consider journaling how your children felt while serving and what they learned.

Two of my daughters recently returned from a mission trip to the Dominican Republic. On the trip, one of the questions they were asked was, "Why were you born in the United States?" What a deep and powerful question to ask your children. What other thought-provoking and age-appropriate questions could you ask? You may want to ask something as simple as, "Who else have you helped this week?" or "Who has helped you this week?"

You could also include notes on what you loved about the service project or what didn't quite work for you. When you revisit the service project, you will have these notes to help make the service project a greater experience and more impactful.

Christian Terms (aka Christianese)

Some of the Christian terms used in this book might be unfamiliar to you. To provide clarity, I have included meanings for several of these terms.

Living water:

This term is used to describe being filled with the Holy Spirit of God, which dwells within everyone who puts their faith and trust in Jesus Christ.

John 4:13-15 says, "Jesus said to her, 'Everyone who drinks of this water will be thirsty again, but whoever drinks of the water that I will give him will never be thirsty again. The water that I will give him will become in him a spring of water welling up to eternal life.' The woman said to him, 'Sir, give me this water, so that I will not be thirsty or have to come here to draw water.'"

The Great Commission:

This term refers to God commanding believers to go and make disciples of all nations.

Matthew 28:18-20 says, "And Jesus came and said to them, 'All authority in heaven and on earth has been given to me. Go therefore and make disciples of all nations, baptizing them in the name of the Father and of the Son and of the Holy Spirit, teaching them to observe all that I have commanded you. And behold, I am with you always, to the end of the age.'"

Saving faith:

This term refers to trusting in Jesus Christ alone for eternal life. This term is not to be confused with temporary faith, which is trusting in Jesus Christ for certain areas of your life or during certain times.

Savior and Lord:

These terms are referring to Jesus Christ. For a Christian, Jesus is their Savior, having saved them from their sins. He is also their Lord, as leader of their life.

Share your faith:

This term refers to telling others about Jesus and how they came to know for certain they have eternal life.

The Gospel or The Good News:

This term refers to the story of Jesus Christ. God sent His Son, Jesus Christ, who lived a perfect life, to pay the penalty for everyone's sins by dying on the cross and raising to life again. All who turn and trust in Him will be forgiven of their sins, reconciled with God, and spend eternity with Him in heaven.

1

Serving in Your Home

> *"Whatever you do, work heartily, as for the Lord and not for men,"* **Colossians 3:23**

Let's Talk:
When attempting to come up with ways to introduce serving others to our children, we don't need to look any further than our own home. Serving God and others starts by serving within our family. Let's talk with our children about the countless opportunities to serve with a loving heart within our home.

For this service project, younger children may be more receptive to the idea of serving others daily in their home, as they typically have a natural enthusiasm for helping their mom and dad. As our children get older, however, this enthusiasm is usually replaced with a feeling of missing out on something more exciting.

If you notice that your child lacks the joy to serve, don't be discouraged; be consistent to instill the value of serving in your children for their own good and ultimately God's glory.

Let's Prep:
Create a list of things for your children to do around the house to help others. You may want to include things different from their regular daily chores (i.e., making the bed, brushing teeth, etc.).

Let's Serve:
Talk with your children about the importance of serving others in your home and allow them to help create a list of ways to bless others living under their same roof. Pick a couple of tasks, get started, and come together as a family to talk about your experience once all the duties are finished. Ask questions like, "How did it feel to serve those closest to you?" or "If someone did something for you, how does it feel to be served?"

In moving forward, take the time to verbally reward those who continue to serve others in your home. One way our family has made serving at home more exciting is to call out those who are blessing others during family dinner. For example, our daughter, Hannah, might report that she saw Sarah make Elizabeth's bed in the morning. In response, we might say, "Good job, Sarah! Thanks for doing that for your sister!"

With only a few simple words, we acknowledge and recognize the behaviors we want to continue seeing in our children. A little recognition truly does go a long way to encourage each child and help this form of serving others continue.

Let's Pray:

Father God, we thank You for the opportunity to serve those living in our home. We ask that You give us opportunities daily to make a difference in the lives of others as we ultimately seek to glorify You. In the name of Jesus, we pray. Amen.

Let's Reflect:

2

Serving the Homeless

> *"For I was hungry and you gave me food, I was thirsty and you gave me drink, I was a stranger and you welcomed me,"*
> **Matthew 25:35**

Let's Talk:

The topic of homelessness can be difficult for even adults to navigate. How can we explain this complicated and often misunderstood social issue to our children while instilling compassion and empathy for our neighbors suffering with homelessness?

I think it is important for us first to look at what we may already be conveying to our children based on our current attitude towards homelessness. When you see someone on the side of the road, what is your first reaction? Do you roll up the car window, lock the door, and try to avoid eye contact? Is that person on the side of the road greeted with a smile, wave, and possibly some money or a gift card for food?

Let's talk with our children of all ages about how to serve homeless neighbors while encouraging a servant's heart.

Let's Prep:

Collect the following items. Be sure to gather enough items so that each person serving has at least one of each item.

» Plastic zipper bags

» A pair of men's socks

» Mini-toiletries (i.e., deodorant, foot powder, lotion)

» Non-perishable snacks (i.e., beef jerky, granola bars, raisins, applesauce)

» Water bottle (during hot months)

» Printed and folded tract from the following website: www.servingtogether.org/printables

Let's Serve:

Talk with your children about homelessness. Explain that homelessness, simply put, is not having a home. It's important to remind your children that being homeless is a circumstance; it is not a person's identity. Explain that the packages you will prepare will not solve all the homeless person's problems. However, every act of kindness matters as we work to build a proper perspective of homelessness.

Begin filling the zipper bags with the items listed above. Encourage your child to take their time when assembling the bags, which will be called Blessing Bags, and remind them that this is a gift and. While the goal is to make the bag as neat as possible, don't focus too much on perfection. A messy bag made with love is far better than a flawless bag made while stressfully seeking perfection.

Use this time to continue discussing homelessness and pray for the person who will be receiving the Blessing Bag. You may want to take this project a step further and include a card or personal note to let the recipient know that you care for and are praying for them! When your family has finished assembling the bags, store them in your car and prayerfully wait for an opportunity to bless someone in need.

Let's Pray:
Father God, thank You for the examples provided in the Bible, which lead us to love and care for our homeless neighbors. Bless us with wisdom and discernment as we lead our children to put others before themselves. Prepare the hearts of those who will receive the Blessing Bags. May they truly feel Your love for them through this act of kindness. In the name of Jesus, we pray. Amen.

Let's Reflect:

3

Thank Our Troops

"Greater love has no one than this, that someone lay down his life for his friends." John 15:13

Let's Talk:

As Americans, we enjoy amazing freedoms daily. However, these freedoms come with a cost. Brave men and women in the armed services leave the comforts of home and family behind to serve throughout the world and put their lives on the line for our freedoms.

A Million Thanks is a nonprofit organization that provides support and appreciation to active and veteran members of our military services through letters. Let's talk with our children about the sacrifice that members of our military make, taking this opportunity to thank them for their commitment and bravery though cards, letters, and prayers.

Let's Prep:

Gather supplies to make cards, such as card stock, scissors, glue, markers, stickers, etc.

Let's Serve:

Explain to your children the primary purpose of our military: to serve and protect our country. Talk with them about how many of the places military members must go are far away from their homes and how hard it must be for these men and women to be away from their families. If you are a military family, your children will likely already understand these concepts personally.

Later, explain that one way your family can encourage these brave men and women is by sending letters and cards from people in their home country. Here are some guidelines when writing your letters or cards:

» A Million Thanks does not accept store-bought cards

» Do not include an envelope

» Be sure to keep the letter positive and avoid politics

» Offer support and thank military members for their selfless service

» It's okay to talk about yourself (i.e., hobbies, family, school, pets, sports, etc.)

» Feel free to include your name and address; the recipient may respond

» Letters can be any length; just make sure your words are heartfelt

» Glitter or confetti is not allowed

» Be sure to send holiday cards a few months in advance to allow time for delivery

» Include uplifting and encouraging quotes and Bible verses

Benita Koeman, a military spouse and founder of the non-denominational Christian ministry "Operation We Are Here," has put together a wonderful list of encouraging Bible verses for our troops. These verses are great to include in your letters and cards.

Here are some encouraging Bible verses to consider including in your cards and letters:

Deuteronomy 31:8	Psalm 55:22
Joshua 1:9	Psalm 89:21
Psalm 4:8	Psalm 91
Psalm 9:9	Psalm 139:7-10
Psalm 23:4	Isaiah 41:10
Psalm 31:14-15	Isaiah 43:1-2
Psalm 32:7-8	Matthew 11:28-29
Psalm 33:20-22	Philippians 4:6-7
Psalm 46:1	Philippians 4:13

Once your cards and letter are finished, send them to A Million Thanks at the following address:

A Million Thanks
17853 Santiago Blvd, #107-355
Villa Park, CA 92861

Prayerfully consider making a small donation to help this organization deliver cards like yours. You can donate as little as $5 through their website: www.amillionthanks.org

Let's Pray:
Father God, we thank You for the brave men and women who risk their lives to serve and defend us and preserve our freedoms. May these cards and letters be encouraging to them, and may they point the service member to You. May service members seek You for refuge, and may You strengthen and protect them. To You be the glory. In the name of Jesus, we pray. Amen.

Let's Reflect:

4

Showing Gratitude to the Overlooked

> *"Rejoice always, pray without ceasing, give thanks in all circumstances; for this is the will of God in Christ Jesus for you."* 1 Thessalonians 5:16-18

Let's Talk:

Showing our appreciation and gratitude for firefighters, paramedics, and police officers often comes naturally to us. However, there are many others doing jobs that are vitally essential to our daily lives. Some of these jobs include trash collectors, letter carriers, construction workers, custodians, and many others. When thinking about jobs deserving our appreciation and gratitude, these jobs are often overlooked.

Let's talk with our children about how to recognize and show gratitude to people with these underappreciated jobs.

Let's Prep:

Required Items:

- » Stationary or paper for making letters and cards, including stickers, stamps, and other items

- » Printed and folded tract from the following website: www.servingtogether.org/printables

- » Church information, including service times and locations

- » Gift card to a local restaurant, cold bottles of water, store-bought or homemade cookies, or other small tokens of appreciation

Let's Serve:

Talk with your children about which careers they feel would likely be underappreciated on a regular basis. Decide together who your family would like to acknowledge and thank.

Next, make thank you cards and letters. Let the recipient know how thankful you are for how they serve through their job. Feel free to include Bible verses and a Good News tract to point them to God. Decide if a small gift would be appropriate.

It is best to include your children as much as possible. They can help with making the cookies, putting the water bottles in the refrigerator, and participating in whatever ways are appropriate to each child. Be creative and have fun! You may want to hand-deliver your cards with a big smile or acknowledge someone secretly. Whatever you choose, let your light shine to brighten their day.

Let's Pray:

Lord, we ask You to bless these hard-working, underappreciated individuals. Lord, may our children grow to see people differently, as You do. May they grow to see people as being created in Your image, including those often overlooked by society. Lord, we pray Your love is clearly displayed to these people through our acknowledgements and gratitude. We pray they come to know Your love in a real and personal way through saving faith. In the name of Jesus, we pray. Amen.

Let's Reflect:

5

Mercy House Global

"The steadfast love of the Lord never ceases; his mercies never come to an end; they are new every morning; great is your faithfulness." **Lamentations 3:22-23**

Let's Talk:

Of all the research conducted to write this book, becoming aware of the plight facing many women and teen girls in the slums of Kenya has been hardest for me. While learning about the extreme poverty in Kenya, I discovered that most families in the slums are unemployed and unable to earn a living. As a result, many young girls are being pressured into prostitution by their own families to earn money.

These girls risk their lives as prostitutes to receive the equivalent of a couple dollars at most. They often end up with diseases, experience pregnancy at an early age, and have a continued sense of hopelessness. Many girls even die due to health complications, resulting from dangerous "back alley" abortion attempts.

Mercy House Global is a Christ-centered nonprofit organization that started with a God-given desire to rescue pregnant teens from these desperate situations.

"Mercy House exists to engage, empower, and disciple women around the globe in Jesus' name. We provide for the rescue of pregnant girls in Kenya and provide a home for them. We empower their families and many others with dignified work so we can redeem future generations. We do this by engaging those with resources to say yes to the plight of women in poverty by empowering women around the world through partnerships and sustainable fair trade product development." (mercyhouseglobal.org)

Let's talk with our children about how we can support the efforts of Mercy House Global through a simple purchase. I am so excited to see the Lord use this project to make an eternal difference in the lives of impoverished, oppressed women around the world through Mercy House Global.

Let's Prep:

Purchase do-it-yourself bracelet kits from the following website: www.servingtogether.org/braceletkit. You can order as many or as few kits as you desire online, but I suggest planning for at least two bracelets per person. One bracelet will be for your child to keep. You can use the other bracelet to give away and raise awareness with others.

Optional:

In addition to purchasing the bracelet kits, consider checking out their online marketplace https://shop.mercyhouseglobal. org/ to see many other trendy fair-trade products and the "Fair-Trade Friday" box, which contains 3 to 4 hand-selected fair-trade products.

Let's Serve:

The thought of discussing a topic like this with your children in an age-appropriate way may seem overwhelming. I suggest starting the conversation by talking about poverty. You could begin by telling your children about the women in Kenya and how they are struggling to care for their families.

Next, discuss how Mercy House Global is helping these women by equipping them with a trade, while also providing a way for people to help support these women and families through the purchasing of their unique crafts.

> *"When you purchase our fair trade product, you are empowering survivors and those at-risk to be trafficked." - Mercy House Global website*

Once your "do-it-yourself bracelet kits" arrive, they will include an instruction card on how to prepare the bracelet. Depending on your child's age and physical ability, they may need more help than others to make the bracelet.

When your child has finished, they can choose to keep their bracelet or gift it to someone else. As people notice and comment on your bracelets, you and your children can use the conversation as an opportunity to share some information about the women who made these beads and how your purchase has truly made a difference in their lives!

Let's Pray:

Dearest God, we thank You for Mercy House Global and their desire to rescue these women, teach them a trade, and share the enduring hope found in Jesus Christ alone! Please continue to bless their ministry abundantly and protect them as they seek to liberate the captives from physical and spiritual bondage. Soften our hearts and the hearts of our children to see the world around them through Your eyes. Align the desires of our hearts with Your will, enabling us to make an eternal impact on the lives of these women for Your glory and their good. In the name of Jesus, we pray. Amen.

Let's Reflect:

6

Caring for the Elderly in our Neighborhood

> *"Do not cast me off in the time of old age; forsake me not when my strength is spent."* **Psalm 71:9**

Let's Talk:

As we teach our children to honor their elders, most of us have lots of opportunities in our own neighborhoods. Let's talk with our children about seeking opportunities to get to know and serve our elderly neighbors.

Not all of our elderly neighbors need help, as many are healthy, active, and independent. On the flip side, other seniors who have always been independent now find it hard to ask for assistance. Your children can help ease any reluctance in an elderly person by simply allowing them to see their genuine desire to serve them.

Let's Prep:

Make a list of a few elderly neighbors that could benefit from a helping hand. Choose people who live within walking distance. Decide if you prefer helping someone you already know or if you desire to use this as an opportunity to reach out and meet new people. Once you have decided on which neighbor to help, it's time to get your children involved.

With your children, consider the time of year and season when offering to help. You might be able to provide suggestions to your neighbor, such as weeding or raking leaves. Maybe you could start off small by asking if you could pick anything up while you are out. If your neighbor is still mostly independent, you may choose to bake them a treat or invite them over for dinner. Create a plan with your children that works for your family.

Here are some service ideas:

- » Raking
- » Picking up sticks
- » Mowing the lawn
- » Weeding
- » Shoveling snow
- » Cooking dinner or dessert
- » Running errands
- » Providing company
- » Asking for prayer requests
- » Changing lightbulbs, smoke detector batteries, etc.

Let's Serve:

It's game time. If you haven't gotten to know your elderly neighbor, step one is meeting them. If you have both been neighbors for a while, you might feel uncomfortable knocking on their door to meet them. Feel free to let it happen naturally the next time you and your children see that person outside. Approach them and introduce yourself and your family. Remember, your child's charm will oftentimes make it far less awkward for everyone.

No matter how you choose to serve the elderly in your community, be sure the focus is not only teaching your children to honor the elders, but also to share God's love with them. Find opportunities to share your faith with your newfound friends. Invite them to attend a service or a special event at your church. As you and your children pray for your neighbor, be sure to pray that God receives the credit for the love you are sharing, which He first gave us. Pray that through this act of love they would come to have a saving faith.

Let's Pray:

Dearest God, we thank You for the ability to serve our elderly neighbors. We pray our honor, love, and service for them would point them to You. Continue to instill in our children a heart to serve others and a desire to make the gospel known everywhere we go. May we lead by example as we also learn to love others more than ourselves. In the name of Jesus, we pray. Amen.

Let's Reflect:

7

Serving on the Road

"For you were called to freedom, brothers. Only do not use your freedom as an opportunity for the flesh, but through love serve one another. For the whole law is fulfilled in one word: 'You shall love your neighbor as yourself.'" **Galatians 5:13-14**

Let's Talk:

As you have seen in this book, serving others doesn't start and end in your home, your neighborhood, your state, or even your country. We can serve others anytime and anywhere. As we begin to develop a heart for serving others as parents, our children will often develop the same type of heart.

This week, let's talk to our children about finding opportunities to serve others while being out of town. Whether it's for a weekend at the lake or an entire week at the beach, find ways to serve those around you everywhere you go.

Let's Prep:

No preparation is required.

Let's Serve:

Serving others should become a natural part our lives, bringing joy to you and those being served. There is no need to take a vacation from serving others. During vacations, have your children look for quick, but meaningful ways to serve others. This can be as easy as holding the door open for someone, letting someone go ahead of you in line (especially when their hands are full), helping someone who dropped something, or greeting others with a big smile.

As you're traveling with your children, ask them who they've helped and who have they noticed helping others. These questions aren't intended for self-gratification, but they intend to encourage excitement and good habits in your children to last a lifetime. Always point your children to the gospel to better understand the reason to serve others. If our goal is not the gospel, our impact will fall drastically short and will be ultimately meaningless.

Let's Pray:

We thank You, God, for this time away from home and our regular routine. We pray, Father God, for each person we have and will encounter, whom we were able to serve in some small way. We pray each one of them will have seen the love of Christ in us and ultimately that they, too, would come to know and love Christ Jesus as their Savior and Lord. In the name of Jesus, we pray. Amen.

Let's Reflect:

8

Volunteering Where You Are Planted

"So then, as we have opportunity, let us do good to everyone, and especially to those who are of the household of faith." **Galatians 6:10**

Let's Talk:

As we read this book and begin to foster a heart of service in our children, it is important to see the opportunities to serve around us every week at our church. Each church will have unique opportunities for you and your family to serve, but not all service opportunities will be age-appropriate for your children. Consider looking for something easy to do with your children, such as serving in a Sunday school class or volunteering in the nursery once a month. The important thing is to make it a routine — something that your children will count on doing on a regular basis.

Our daughter, Hannah, has been serving with the children's ministry at our church since she was 5 years old. On many occasions, she served with children much older than her. This has never bothered her in the least. She has served with them at summer camps, Bible studies, etc. When the children's ministry sent out a Christmas card with a picture of all the adult volunteers, she wondered why she hadn't been included on the photo. That is how invested she is as a volunteer in our church's children's ministry.

Hannah is now 9 years old and has some of her older siblings join her in serving. For Hannah, serving at our church each week is a part of life that she takes great pride in doing. The benefits from regular volunteering is enormous. As your children get older, they will begin to feel like part of a team and more invested in the church they attend.

Let's talk about regular volunteer work that will be appropriate for your family. The goal isn't to add another task to your family's never-ending to-do list. Rather, my hope is for God to use these service opportunities to mold our hearts and the hearts of our children, causing these experiences to be joyful and wonderful for those serving and being served.

Let's Prep:
Prayerfully, pick an area where you would be interested in serving alongside your children at your church. Be sure to find out the service requirements, such as a background check, fingerprinting, etc.

Speak with the volunteer coordinator and ask to try it out one week with your children. There's no reason to start out with a long-term commitment until you find out where you fit in best.

Then, try it out! Before bringing the little one, try it out first to better know what to expect and have ideas on how your children can help!

If you don't have a church you attend regularly, this is a great time to find one. As you decide which church to attend, be sure to research the church; all churches are most certainly not the same. For tips on finding a Bible-teaching church in your area, visit our website: www.servingtogether.org/resoures

If you're looking for a short-term volunteer opportunity, consider volunteering for a week in the summer at a local Vacation Bible School (VBS). This could even become a family tradition.

Let's Serve:

Once you have your game plan, enthusiastically tell your children what you will be doing. Explain exactly what to expect and why their jobs are important. Whether it's picking up toys, handing out snacks (for younger children), helping with puppets, or reading a Bible story, each role is equally important. You will quickly find that your children will begin asking you to go to church on Sundays instead of the other way around.

Let's Pray:

Dear God, we thank You for the opportunity to become a more active part of the body of believers where we worship. We pray our children will continue to build a love for serving, being a light in our church for others to see. Use our family's service to encourage other families to serve, too. May all we do bring glory, not to ourselves, but to You. In the name of Jesus, we pray. Amen.

Let's Reflect:

9

Honoring the Elderly

Let's Talk:

In today's culture, having respect for our elders does not always come naturally. As Christians, we recognize our responsibility to treat our elders with dignity and honor. However, the next generation needs to understand the importance of honor and love, especially for our elders. Honor is simply to respect, value, and esteem.

In *Saying Goodbye to Whining, Complaining, and Bad Attitudes … in You and Your Kids*, Dr. Scott Turansky and Joanne Miller say, "Honor thinks what would please someone else, and gives more than is expected. It's putting someone else's needs above your own. Honor values others in tangible ways."

This week, let's talk with our children about activities to help us love and honor the elders in our community. Whether it's someone we know or a stranger, the objective is to love and honor them, demonstrating Christ's love in word and action.

Let's Prep:
Gather card-making supplies, such as card stock, scissors, glue, markers, ribbon, stickers, rubber stamps, etc.

Contact a local nursing home or two. Find out about their upcoming events and ask if your family could bring cards or letters for the residents. Also, find out how many residents might be in attendance. This will help you determine the number of cards your family should make.

Save the date and time in your calendar. If you're anything like me, this step could easily slip through the cracks.

Let's Serve:
Talk with your children about the elderly. One easy way for your children to learn to honor the elderly is by watching and hearing how you treat the elderly. As you model a Christ-like example of love and respect, you can talk with your children about true biblical love on display. "We love because He first loved us." 1 John 4:19

Next, it's time to make the cards. Whether it's for St. Patrick's Day, Valentine's Day, or Christmas, have fun! As you and your children think of kind things to say, be sure to include Scripture verses to encourage and share the Good News of salvation through Jesus. We want every service project to point back to God because it's all being done for His glory!

Before the delivery day, talk with your children about things they may see at the nursing home. From oxygen tanks to wheelchairs, little ones often do better when they know what to expect. Delivering the cards will likely be exciting for everyone involved; children tend to love the elderly, and the elderly are usually captivated by children and ecstatic to have visitors. Allow your children to hand out the letters and talk with folks as your time and comfort level permits.

Lastly, talk about the positive aspects of your visit as a family and decide if it's something you'd like to do for the next holiday. This fun service project is worth repeating and can help develop hearts to honor the elderly in our children.

Let's Pray:
Father God, we pray for our children to have a heart for the elderly. We pray that they would honor and respect the elderly and others in their lives. Help us show the love of Christ to others as we strive to put others before ourselves, setting an example for our children. May the elderly we served this week see Christ in us. For those who don't know You, we pray they come to know and love You as their Savior and Lord. In the name of Jesus, we pray. Amen.

Let's Reflect:

10

Feed My Starving Children

"He upholds the cause of the oppressed and gives food to the hungry." **Psalm 146:7 (NIV)**

Let's Talk:

There are millions of children around the world who don't have enough food to live a healthy lifestyle. More than 3 million children each year die from undernourishment. Feed My Starving Children (FMSC) is a Christian nonprofit organization that has a mission to "feed God's starving children hungry in body and spirit." Yearly, FMSC addresses this massive crisis by shipping millions of volunteer-packed, nutritious meals to approximately 70 countries. Each vitamin-and-mineral fortified rice meal, also known as a "MannaPack," costs less than 25 cents to produce. These meals are shipped to FMSC partner missions and humanitarian organizations who distribute them daily to orphanages, schools, clinics, and feeding programs in areas where disaster, poverty, disease, and other circumstances prevent regular access to nutritious food. With God's help and the support of others, FMSC strives to eliminate starvation in children throughout the world.

"Hope begins with nutritious food. FMSC exists to provide this hope in the name of Jesus. Nutrition allows children to grow, thrive and develop to their full potential so that they can become productive members of their communities." (www.fmsc.org)

Let's Prep:
Feed My Starving Children has locations in Arizona, Illinois, Minnesota, and Texas. In addition, they have hundreds of mobile packing events each year in locations throughout the United States. If your children are 5 years of age or older, you can visit their website (www.fmsc.org) and find the date of the next packing event in your area.

If you find an event in your area and are available to participate, simply make the necessary preparations to attend with your family. If you aren't able to participate at one of their events, your family can still do the project below.

You will need the following supplies:

>> One small tube of M&M MINIS candy per person. These can be purchased at many convenience stores or by visiting www.fmscmarketplace.org.

>> At least one roll of quarters

Additional preparations:
Prepare a chart or list of things your children can do to earn quarters in and around the house. Be creative and have fun with this part. The chores should be different from your child's

everyday routine. For young children, draw pictures or use clip art when making your list.

Let's Serve:

Start this service project on a sweet note by enjoying some M&M MINIS candy with your children. After all, your children will need empty tubes to start earning and collecting quarters. Talk with your children about world hunger and let them ask questions. It will be helpful to share some facts about FMSC, including their mission and their ultimate goal.

Next, explain that each empty M&M mini-tube can hold 56 quarters, which is $14. FMSC calls these containers of quarters "Mission Money." Remember, each meal FMSC provides costs less than 25 cents per child. By filling one M&M mini-tube with quarters, your family can help FMSC provide a hungry child with 56 nutritious meals.

Then, explain the list of chores available to earn quarters and have each child pick chores from the list. When your family has finished filling each M&M mini-tube with quarters, pray with your children for the children throughout the world who will receive this much-needed food. Once the project is finished, send your donations to FMSC. You are welcome to donate any amount you desire. If you are near one of the FMSC locations, you can drop off filled tubes at any location. To find a FMSC location, visit www.fmscmarketplace.org/pages/store-locations.

If you are not near an FMSC location, donations can be mailed to the following address:

FMSC
401 93rd Ave NW
Coon Rapids, MN 55433

Let's Pray:

Dear God, we thank You for our daily bread. Lord, please use our donations to feed children physically, but even more importantly, to feed them spiritually. Cause our contribution, no matter how little, to make a huge impact for Your glory. In the name of Jesus, we pray. Amen.

Let's Reflect:

11

Praying

"do not be anxious about anything, but in everything by prayer and supplication with thanksgiving let your requests be made known to God. And the peace of God, which surpasses all understanding, will guard your hearts and your minds in Christ Jesus." **Philippians 4:6-7**

Let's Talk:

When most people think of serving others, praying is usually not the first thing to come to mind. Often, we feel that serving must be doing something tangible. However, prayer is one of the most powerful ways to serve. Like everything else we do as parents, our children are looking to us for an example to follow.

When we make prayer our go-to response, we are inviting God to intervene and intercede. We are also teaching our children to pray for the big things and the small things in our lives — and in the lives of others. As prayer shifts from a routine to a natural response, our children will grow to know the God who hears our prayers and is able to do exceedingly more than we could ask or imagine.

In the Bible, we are given countless examples of how God has moved in response to prayer to accomplish His will. God desires us to pray to Him about all things because He loves us and wants each of us to experience life to the fullest through a close relationship with Him. I pray that we never underestimate the power of serving others through prayer.

No matter the size of the issue, we can always pray! There are no age limits, no preparation required, and no special skills needed. Our children can serve through prayer at any time and in any place. This week, let's talk with our children about how to serve others through prayer.

Let's Prep:

No preparation is required.

Let's Serve:

Your children are never too young to start laying the groundwork. Even children who are not old enough to speak are often listening and paying attention to their surroundings. When your children are praying, don't worry about them doing it exactly "right." The goal is to help your children understand the importance of prayer and make it part of normal, everyday life.

Start by talking with your children about the awesome privilege of prayer. Explain that prayer is simply talking to God and that He desires for us to pray to Him no matter how big or small.

Feel free to share personal examples of prayers from your own life and God's responses to your prayers.

One of the easiest ways to teach your children to pray is by modeling it in your own life. When you eat, before bed or when hearing about the needs of others, pray aloud with your children to help them learn by your example. You can also remember to include prayer as a part of every service project your family is doing together. As you continue serving others through prayer, look forward to having a front row seat to God's gracious and occasionally miraculous responses!

Let's Pray:
Father God, we thank You for giving us the privilege to bring our requests directly to You through prayer. We know that You hear our prayers and answer each one according to Your will and great faithfulness. Please, help each child understand the importance of praying in all circumstances. Help us begin to use prayer more and more as a way to serve others each and every day. In the name of Jesus, we pray. Amen.

Let's Reflect:

12

Giving in Secret

> *"But when you give to the needy, do not let your left hand know what your right hand is doing, so that your giving may be in secret. And your Father who sees in secret will reward you."*
> *Matthew 6:3-4*

Let's Talk:

Whether it's buying someone a gift or giving money to the homeless, giving to others can often cause us to feel good. The giving doesn't even have to be monetary. It could be raking someone's yard or giving them a card when they don't feel well. These acts of giving our time and money are certainly a blessing to those receiving the generosity, and recognition is usually given to the person on the giving end.

This recognition can cause us to feel good about ourselves for blessing others, and there is nothing wrong with feeling good when doing good. For this service project, however, we are going to remove the possibility for recognition when giving by focusing on giving in secret. Let's talk with our children about the desire to bless others without getting any credit or recognition.

Let's Prep:

Print and fold a tract from the following website: www. servingtogether.org/printables Depending on what you can afford and which activity you choose to do, you will also need between $2 and $20 for this service project. You may want to allow your children to do chores for extra money to help them really take ownership of this project.

Let's Serve:

Talk with your children about what it means to give in secret and allow them to brainstorm ways to secretly bless another person. It can be something as simple as leaving quarters at the laundromat, adding extra coins to expired parking meters, or paying it backward and treating the person behind you to dinner at the drive-through. Be creative and have fun! Be sure to leave the printed foldable track behind so God will receive all the credit.

Let's Pray:

Dearest Lord, thank You for the opportunity to give to others in secret. May the recipients feel immensely blessed by our acts of kindness, giving You all of the credit and glory. In the name of Jesus, we pray. Amen.

Let's Reflect:

13

Scripture Rock Painting

"He answered, 'I tell you, if these were silent, the very stones would cry out.'" **Luke 19:40**

Let's Talk:

As Christians, we should encourage one another and build each other up, and there are so many ways to put this into action. This week, let's talk with our children about encouraging others and sharing the gospel with those we know and complete strangers.

Let's Prep:

Gather the following supplies:

> » Acrylic paint

> » Paint brushes

> » Rocks (smooth, large rocks)

> » Newspaper

> » Pencil

> » Permanent marker(s)

> » Clear waterproof sealer

> » Cup of water for brush cleanup

> » Paper towels or cloth rags for spills and cleanup

Let's Serve:

First, ask your children to think of encouraging Bible verses and pictures to paint. You could also look on Pinterest for some fun ideas. Feel free to sketch out their ideas on a piece of paper.

Next, find some rocks. Any rock outside with a flat, long surface works well. If you have a stream or river nearby, start looking there to find smooth, flat stones. You can also purchase rocks at most craft stores and online. The smoother the rock, the easier it will be to paint.

Then, clean the rocks. Using warm soapy water and a scrub brush, you or your children can clean the rocks to prepare them to be painted. After rinsing the soap away, allow the rock to dry completely before beginning to paint.

The following part is fun and easy for children of all ages. Place the dried rocks on a piece of newspaper and paint each one a solid color. You want to paint the rocks one side at a time, allowing time for each side to dry before painting the other side. For the background color, pick a light color for the best results.

After the entire rock is painted and dried, paint a design or picture on one side of the rock. Younger children can smear different colors together to make their masterpiece. Older children may want to sketch out a picture with their pencil first. You may also try using a stencil and sponge to paint a fun design or pattern. When layering colors, always allow the rock to dry completely before painting with the next color.

Once the artwork side of the rock is completely dry, flip the rock over to write an encouraging Bible verse in permanent marker. The size of the rock will determine the length of the Bible verse. You could also use words such as love, believe, John 3:16, etc. to encourage the person finding the rock to look up the Bible verse.

When you and your children are finished, allow the rock to dry for at least 24 hours. Then, apply a clear waterproof topcoat.

The last step is for you and your children to find places to leave the rocks. You can leave some of the rocks for people you know or one in your neighbor's garden. Other rocks can be placed in parks, along walking paths, and almost anywhere rocks can already be found. Pray for those who will find the rocks to be encouraged and to have a desire to seek out the greatest encouragement through the gospel.

"Will you allow the rocks to cry out in your place? Go ahead and let your painted rocks cry out...But make sure you don't forget to praise Him too!" – Lil from Embracing the Lovely

Let's Pray:

Lord, we pray You are glorified through every service project we do. Please, use these small acts of encouragement to point those in our community to You through the gospel. In the name of Jesus, we pray. Amen.

Let's Reflect:

14

Loving God's Animals

"For every beast of the forest is mine, the cattle on a thousand hills. I know all the birds of the hills, and all that moves in the field is mine." **Psalm 50:10-11**

Let's Talk:

For many of us, pets are considered an important part of our family. Whether it is a dog, cat, bird or fish, we love these animals both large and small. We may feel like we "own" our pets; however, the Bible teaches that these and all animals belong to God. Just like other things God created in nature, we are stewards of these things.

"And God said, 'Let the earth bring forth living creatures according to their kinds —livestock and creeping things and beasts of the earth according to their kinds.'" And it was so. And God made the beasts of the earth according to their kinds and the livestock according to their kinds, and everything that creeps on the ground according to its kind. And God saw that it was good." **Genesis 1:24-25**

Like many things God created, He said the animals were good. God cares for all His creation, including animals. God desires our families to care for His creation, too.

For this service project, let's talk with our children about how to honor animals, another one of God's creations.

Let's Prep:
Before the project, collect some of the following items:

» Several old t-shirts

» Scissors

» Printed and folded tract from the following website: www.servingtogether.org/printables

» Address for a local animal rescue shelter

Optional:

» Old towels, blankets, and pillows

Let's Serve:
As a family, discuss ways to honor God's creation, specifically animals. Explain that animals ultimately belong to God, and we are caretakers of them. As a family, praise God for His amazing creation.

Visit our website to print easy-to-follow instructions on how to make a no-sew dog chew toy. For young children, please cut up the t-shirt beforehand or allow them to start working on coloring a card while you cut out the pieces. Lastly, bag up your cards and toys and drop them off at a local animal rescue.

Let's Pray:

Father God, we thank You for everything You have created for our enjoyment and stewardship. Help us to be faithful stewards and guide us as we teach our children to care for animals in ways honoring to You. May our actions reflect Your love. In the name of Jesus, we pray. Amen.

Let's Reflect:

15

Angel Tree

> *"Whoever is generous to the poor lends to the Lord, and he will repay him for his deed." Proverbs 19:17*

Let's Talk:

Salvation Army's Angel Tree program was created in 1979. That year, it provided gifts to more than 700 children. Each year, Angel Tree provides new clothes and gifts to approximately 1 million children who do not usually receive gifts at Christmas.

While the world is telling us that "Christmas is a season of giving," and our children are hearing "Christmas is a season of receiving," let's take the opportunity to point them to the One who gave it all — Jesus.

As Christians, Christmas is the time when we celebrate the birth of Jesus. Let's use this opportunity to model and teach our children to be intentional about looking beyond our own desires and doing what we can to meet the needs of others. Angel Tree is a great way to bring the needs of others into focus; it also provides a practical way to help meet their needs.

"The Salvation Army celebrates the reason for the season by sharing Christ's hope, love, and joy with low-income families. Our Christmas toy donations and financial assistance are a direct response to God's call to care for the poor, hungry, sick, and displaced. From providing family dinners and keeping the heater on to putting toys under the Christmas tree, lending a hand with holiday events, and offering healing and hope through spiritual guidance, we help with Christmas by giving gifts that serve the body, mind, and soul." – **Salvation Army USA**

Let's Prep:

Starting in early November, you can find Angel Trees with Angel Tags located in various locations, including state and federal buildings, malls, retail stores, and churches. After finding an Angel Tree location, decide how many "angels" your family would like to adopt. The average cost to purchase most or all items on a child's wish list is approximately $50.

Let's Serve:

While talking to your children about the excitement of Christmas morning, explain that many families are unable to bless their children with gifts. Some families must choose between buying gifts to put under the tree and putting food on the table or paying for water and heat.

The Salvation Army's Angel Tree program creates opportunities for families like yours to help families in need during the Christmas season. Let your children know that each family receiving gifts will hear about the best gift ever given, which is really why we celebrate Christmas.

Visit a local Angel Tree with your children and pull one or more Angel Tags from the tree. Each tag will have basic information about the child, including their age, gender, clothing size, and a gift wish list. Note that some of the requested gifts are expensive, such as bikes or video game systems. Talk with your children before picking an angel to discuss any budget set for this project.

Purchase some or all items and simply return the gifts to the location where you received the tag. One mom of four children recommends making this a special shopping trip in which the focus is choosing a gift for the angel and not making it part of your other shopping. Taking this additional step can make the service project more impactful.

The Salvation Army will distribute the gifts to the family a few days before Christmas. This can make Christmas morning even more exciting for the children and can show the love of Christ to the parents.

"Every child deserves to experience the joy of Christmas morning." –**The Salvation Army's Angel Tree program**

Let's Pray:
Dear God, thank You for another opportunity to demonstrate Your love to others by blessing these less fortunate families and

their children during the Christmas season. May the families receiving these gifts have open hearts as they hear the true Christmas story. May they come to receive the greatest gift through Jesus, being forever changed for Your glory and their good. In the name of Jesus, we pray. Amen.

Let's Reflect:

16

Become an Organ Donor

> *"And I will give you a new heart, and a new spirit I will put within you. And I will remove the heart of stone from your flesh and give you a heart of flesh."* **Ezekiel 36:26**

Let's Talk:

I had never really given much thought to becoming an organ donor. For me, it was just a box to consider checking when applying for a driver's license. After I met a 6-year-old boy named Landon, all of that changed. At a young age, Landon had a heart attack. To help him stay alive, he received an implanted artificial heart pump. This temporary solution would help him survive while he awaited a new heart from an organ donor.

This may sound simple until realizing that the donated heart couldn't come from an adult who checked a box while getting a new driver's license. Instead, the donated heart must come from another child, being roughly the same age and size as Landon.

Thinking about pediatric organ donation can be extremely difficult. It is far more difficult for parents to decide on pediatric organ donation in the midst of a tragedy. If this topic isn't discussed before something unthinkable occurs, we might miss the enormous blessing of giving life to children in desperate need. It is hard to imagine a greater final act of generosity and service.

Let's Prep:

Parents, take some time to discuss your views on organ donation as a couple before gathering your children. Pray together and ask God to give you wisdom and guidance. You may have many unanswered questions about this infrequently discussed topic, so feel free to visit www.organdonor.gov or www.donatelife.net for more details. While on the website, take a minute and write down current facts to use as encouragement for educating your children on this topic.

If you decide against moving forward with organ donation, this is still a great opportunity to discuss and pray about what organ donation means for your family.

Let's Serve:

As you start this discussion with your children, consider the age of your children and start by asking age-appropriate questions to discover their current understanding about organ donation. Here are a few suggestions:

> » Where is your heart?

> » Do you know what a liver does?

> » What are our earthly bodies versus heavenly bodies?

» What is an organ donor?

» Who can become an organ donor?

» How is becoming an organ donor related to serving others?

Next, tell them some facts about organ donation. For example, there were nearly 2,000 children under the age of 18 on the national transplant waiting list in 2018. Afford time to listen to their thoughts and concerns, encourage them as they ask questions, and share your thoughts about organ donation.

Regardless of their age, don't worry if your children don't seem to fully understand. The important part is talking about a rarely discussed topic, while also prayerfully deciding if organ donation is another way for your family to serve others.

Let's Pray:
Oh Lord, thank You for getting us through this difficult topic. Please give us the words needed as parents to discuss organ donation with our children and give us the wisdom needed to make the right decision for our family. We pray for the children and their families everywhere awaiting organ donors. We ask that you would be their refuge and strength, a very present help in their troubled times. May they find their hope in You as they await a miracle. In the name of Jesus, we pray. Amen.

Let's Reflect:

17

Soles for Jesus

"How beautiful are the feet of those who preach the good news!"
Romans 10:15b

Let's Talk:

In sub-Saharan Africa, it is estimated that more than 20 million children are without shoes. Barefoot children who are homeless or living in extreme poverty risk injury while searching for food and other items in dumps and abandoned buildings, or while walking through open sewers and contaminated paths. Many serious health conditions start with the feet. Cracks, cuts, and injuries are almost never treated and can lead to serious infections, amputations, and even death.

Wearing shoes lowers the risk of injury and provides protection and safety by reducing the risk of exposure to parasites like hookworms, pathogens, and hazardous substances that affect public health. Owning a pair of shoes also opens the door for children to attend school or work. Sadly, shoes are simply not affordable for those struggling to survive.

Soles For Jesus (SFJ) exists to share the love of Christ by distributing shoes to the underserved in sub-Saharan Africa. In addition to meeting this physical need, SFJ also works to meet a spiritual one. SFJ has developed partnerships with leaders in Africa sharing the same passion to see the gospel message shared throughout Africa. Those receiving shoes hear the message of Jesus and are given a personal copy of the gospel message in their native language. SFJ believes "sharing shoes, along with the message of Jesus Christ, has the power to change a life."

Let's Prep:

For this service project, you will need shoes. However, there is no need to gather them ahead of time.

You will also need paper and craft supplies to make cards or letters.

Let's Serve:

Talk with your children about the tremendous need for shoes in Africa. You can share simple facts and follow up with questions. For example, millions of children in Africa do not have shoes. You can go as deep into these conversations with your children as you determine is appropriate for them. A good way to transition from discussing information about this topic is to ask them if they have any ideas on how to help as a family.

In most homes, you are likely to find many pairs of outgrown or never-worn shoes, belonging to adults and children. Invite your children to help by gathering up these shoes. All shoes are accepted, both new and used shoes, regardless of style or size. Any unwearable shoes will be repurposed, ensuring every pair is used.

Encourage your child to think outside of the box and come up with ways to potentially collect more shoes. Your family could ask neighbors or friends if they are interested in donating any unwanted shoes. Your family may even decide to host a shoe drive. Once all the shoes are gathered, each pair should be bound together as a pair with a rubber band or tied laces. Do not use zip ties.

Next, have your children take a few minutes and create a card or note to share an encouraging message. Each card will be given with a pair of shoes and will be greatly appreciated.

Prayerfully consider including a donation when you send your shoes. While this is not mandatory, a donation goes a long way towards helping SFJ serve those in need. It costs approximately $2 per pair to send the shoes to Africa.

All shoes and monetary donations should be delivered or mailed to the SFJ Milwaukee warehouse at the following address:

Soles For Jesus
8480 N. 87th St.
Milwaukee, WI 53224.

SFJ is a Non-Profit 501(c)(3). For more information about this amazing Christ-centered organization, please visit their website: www.solesforjesus.org.

Let's Pray:

Oh Lord, we thank You for this wonderful opportunity to bless children and families in Africa with shoes. Lord, may these shoes be more than merely a physical provision. We ask You to cause these shoes to serve as a way for many people to find their eternal hope in You. Please, continue to bless the work of Soles For Jesus. Be glorified through what they have done, what they are doing, and what they will do. In the name of Jesus, we pray. Amen.

Let's Reflect:

18

Operation Christmas Child

"So it is not the will of my Father who is in heaven that one of these little ones should perish." Matthew 18:14

Let's Talk:

Many families are familiar with Operation Christmas Child (OCC). It is a project of Samaritan's Purse, an international Christian relief and evangelism organization. The mission of OCC is to demonstrate God's love in a tangible way by collecting shoeboxes filled with school supplies, hygiene items, toys, and notes of encouragement and delivering them to children in need around the world. Since 1993, OCC has collected and delivered more than 168 million shoebox gifts to children in more than 160 countries and territories.

For many of these children, the gift-filled shoebox is the first gift they have ever received. In addition to these shoeboxes, OCC brings the life-changing message of hope through "The Greatest Journey" program, a 12-lesson discipleship program. Children learn from trained, local volunteers what it means to follow Jesus and share their faith with friends and family. Let's excitedly talk with our children about taking part in spreading the gospel of Christ around the world through OCC this year.

Let's Prep:

Gather several items for this project, using the list below as a guide. If you have multiple children, I recommend letting each child make a box. Before purchasing items, allow your children to pick an age and gender. This will help you have a better idea of what to purchase.

For this service project, you will likely want to gather these items with your children. Including your children while picking out the items can help your children feel more invested and connected to the project and the children receiving these shoebox gifts.

Start with an empty medium-sized shoebox. You can use one from your closet, buy a small plastic bin the size of a shoebox, or order a pre-printed shoebox online. Here are some items recommended to fill the shoeboxes:

A "Wow" Item:

» A doll or stuffed animal

» A deflated soccer ball (including a manual air pump to inflate the ball)

» A small musical instrument, such as a harmonica or woodwind recorder

Personal Care Items:

- » comb
- » hairbrush
- » toothbrush
- » washcloth
- » bar soap (packaged and/or in a container)

Clothing and Accessories:

- » shirts and pants
- » underwear
- » shoes and socks
- » flip-flops
- » hat/scarf/mittens
- » sunglasses
- » hair bows
- » friendship bracelets

Crafts and Activities:

- » pencils
- » small manual pencil sharpener
- » colored pencils
- » pencil case
- » crayons
- » markers
- » pens
- » coloring pads
- » coloring books
- » picture book
- » notebooks
- » play dough
- » jump rope

Toys:

> » foam ball

> » kickball (including a manual air pump to inflate the ball)

> » finger puppets

> » slinky

> » interactive toys with push buttons, lights, or noise (including extra batteries)

Let's Serve:

Start by wrapping the box and lid separately in wrapping paper. After all, this is a gift for a special child. Attach the appropriate label to your shoebox, marking if your gift is for a boy or a girl, and select an age category: 2-4, 5-9 or 10-14. The label can be found at the "How to Pack a Shoebox" section at www. servingtogether.org/shoebox. On their website, you can also receive a tracking number to find out where your box will be delivered.

Next, fill the box with the items you have collected. You may want to remove the items from any unnecessary packaging to make more room in the shoebox. You may also want to enclose a note to the child and a photo of your child, your family, or group. If you include your name and an address, the child receiving the shoebox may be able to write back. To avoid unnecessary discouragement, talk to your children about the many reasons the child may not send a letter back to them.

At the beginning of each November, look for Operation Christmas Child shoebox collection centers near you. Throughout the year, you can also build a shoebox online, or mail or drop off your gift-filled shoeboxes to OCC at 801 Bamboo Road, Boone, North Carolina 28607. A suggested donation of $9 per shoebox is essential to help cover shipping costs and other ministry expenses. Lastly, pray for the child who will receive your gift.

Let's Pray:
Dearest God, we thank You for the opportunity to serve with Operation Christmas Child. We ask that you continue to bless this ministry. May many, many more children come to experience Your love and know Your mercy in a real and personal way. In the name of Jesus, we pray. Amen.

Let's Reflect:

19

Sharing Our Faith Through an Act of Kindness

"Go therefore and make disciples of all nations, baptizing them in the name of the Father and of the Son and of the Holy Spirit, teaching them to observe all that I have commanded you. And behold, I am with you always, to the end of the age." **Matthew 28:19-20.**

Let's Talk:

We understand that it is important to teach our children how to read and write, tie their shoes, and, one day, even drive a car. However, teaching them eternal things may not come as naturally. As Christians, we want our families to live out the great commission, but how do we train them to make that a part of their everyday lives?

First, children need to see their parents sharing Christ with others. Children naturally copy their parents, so we need to set an example worth following. Sharing our faith with people around us can be difficult, but it's worth it. Our children need to see us being bold and intentional as we excitedly look for opportunities to share the greatest story ever told with those around us.

Sharing our faith doesn't have to be as hard and scary as it may seem. It doesn't always involve going door-to-door or preaching on a street corner, although sometimes people are called to share in that way. Sharing your faith, even for the smallest child, can be as simple as making a difference through a simple act of kindness. Let's talk with our children about an easy way to share their faith by simply blessing others through a care package.

Let's Prep:
For each person serving, collect at least one of each item listed below:

» Plastic quart-size zipper bag

» Individual-size box or bag of candy (about 3-ounces)

» Travel-size hand sanitizer

» Travel-size hand lotion

» Travel-size tissues

» Travel-size wet wipes

» Gospel tract (print and fold from the following website: www.servingtogether.org/printables

» Information about your church, including service times and locations. If you do not attend a local church, print an invitation for online church from the website

Let's Serve:

Begin preparing the Act of Kindness Blessing Bags. Encourage your children to take their time when assembling each one. Remind them to do their best to neatly organize the items inside the bag, but don't let perfection become the focus. Talk to your children about why it is so important to share their faith with those around them and encourage them to think of people they would like to bless with an Act of Kindness Blessing Bag.

Once the bag is assembled, consider including a card or a note with a favorite Bible verse or a prayer. When you are finished, pray together as a family for those who will receive the Blessing Bags. Then, schedule a time to hand them out. If your child is a little nervous about sharing their faith in this way, let them practice with Christian family members or friends. The encouragement they receive while practicing may be just what they need to get excited about handing out these care packages.

Let's Pray:

Lord, I thank You for this wonderful opportunity to bless others as we learn to boldly share our faith with those around us. Give us a heart for the lost and opportunities to make Your love known to them. Bless each person who receives these gifts with a redemptive heart. In the name of Jesus, we pray. Amen.

Let's Reflect:

20

Free Library

Let's Talk:

Most parents would agree that reading is important. Since our neighborhood library was closed due to remodeling for more than a year, my family decided to become a part of a book-sharing community. Through a family member, a local newspaper company blessed us with an old newspaper dispenser. We painted it, filled it with books, and registered it online for a small one-time fee. The book-sharing community listed our library on their online map, allowing other book lovers to find us.

This week, we will use this creative way to share the gospel and plant seeds within the community around us. I love being able to share books that have made a spiritual impact on me and my children. This little library has been a great way for us to do exactly that in our neighborhood. As a family, talk about the possibility of hosting your own little library. Then, decide if getting and hosting a little library is a good way for your family to bless others while sharing the Good News.

If starting your own free library isn't currently an option for your family, you can still participate in this service project by distributing gospel-centered books with existing little libraries in your community.

Let's Prep:

If you decide to start your own little library, the first step is finding a location for your library. The location should be highly visible and somewhere with a good amount of foot traffic.

Items needed:

» You will need a little library. This is needed to keep the books protected from outside elements. You can either purchase one from www.littlefreelibrary.org or make one yourself. It can be as simple or complex as you want. If you don't have the skills or money to make your library, think outside of the box. Anything that is weatherproof and can hold books can be a library. A large plastic container, an extra mailbox, or even an old mini-refrigerator with a little love could turn out to be a great library.

» You will need books, of course. You can use books that you own and have already read, new books, and books from thrift stores or yard sales. Remember, the primary goal is to have lots of books available that point people to God.

Regardless of whether you decide to start your own little library, print and cut out bookmarks from the following website: www. servingtogether.org/printables. These bookmarks work best when printed on cardstock paper.

Let's Serve:

If your family is ready to start your own little library, take some time to pray with your children, asking the Lord to use your library to make Himself known to many people! Have fun preparing and setting up your little library.

Once your library is up and running, don't forget to provide care and attention. Allow your children to help keep it clean and inviting. As people begin to donate books, place the bookmarks you printed and colored into these books. This is another great way to share God's love with others.

If your family is not ready to start your own little library, consider donating a few books, containing the bookmarks printed during the "Let's Prep" section of this project, to an existing little library in your community. These can be adult or children's books. The important thing is for these books to point people to God.

Let's Pray:

Lord, we are so thankful for the opportunity to bless others and point them towards You. Allow our library to be a blessing and to make Your name known. Prepare the hearts of those who will read these books to be open and receptive. We love You. In the name of Jesus, we pray. Amen.

Let's Reflect:

21

Send College Students Care Packages

> *"Beloved, let us love one another, for love is from God, and whoever loves has been born of God and knows God."* **1 John 4:7**

Let's Talk:

For many college freshmen, living away from home can be an exciting and scary experience. This might be the first time these young adults have been away from home and their normal weekly routines. Mom and dad are neither telling them when to wake nor reminding them to study and do their homework. Their parents are also no longer taking them to church.

Studies estimate between 60 and 80 percent of Christian youth have become disengaged with their faith as they transition to college. For these young students, staying connected to Jesus Christ is so critical, especially during these formative years in college. They will face new challenges and temptations each day, pulling them in many directions. This week, let's talk with our children about how to encourage a college student in their relationship with Christ and cover them in prayer.

Let's Prep:

For this project, you will need the contact information for a college student. Contacting a friend or family member would be a great place to start. You could also contact your church and see if they have someone in mind.

Next, you will need the following supplies to make the care package:

> » Empty box to fill with goodies
>
> » Supplies to make encouraging cards or letters
>
> » Supplies for a care package

Here are some suggestions for goodies to include in the care package. Be creative!

> » Peanut butter to-go pack
>
> » Chips
>
> » Candy
>
> » Multivitamins
>
> » Airborne supplements
>
> » Lip balm
>
> » Travel tissues
>
> » Cups of noodle soup
>
> » Breakfast bars

- » Trail mix

- » Instant mac and cheese

- » School supplies

- » Microwave popcorn

- » Starbucks gift card

- » Simple daily devotional

Let's Serve:

As you prepare the care package, spend time praying with your children for the student who will be receiving your gift. You can also take time to write a letter, encouraging the student to continue seeking God during this season of their life. Allow young children to make a card or color a picture to include. After mailing the package, continue to pray for the student!

Let's Pray:

God, thank You for the opportunity to bless this student. I pray You would use our gift to encourage them and point them to Yourself. Father God, please strengthen and protect this student during this season of life. May this student grow in faith, leaning no longer on the faith of their family, but strengthening a personal faith in Christ Jesus. In the name of Jesus, we pray. Amen.

Let's Reflect:

22

Thanking First Responders

"Greater love has no one than this, that someone lay down his life for his friends." John 15:13

Let's Talk:

Educating your children about first responders and the role they play during an emergency can help provide your children with a sense of security. Talking to your children about emergency situations might feel intimidating because no one wants to think about the worst-case scenario happening. During an emergency, however, it is important for them to understand that there are adults whose job is to help keep them safe.

This week, let's talk with our children about honoring first responders. They risk their lives to save others, and it is important to teach our children to be thankful for these brave men and women.

Let's Prep:

Gather the following items to prepare for this service project:

» Basket or a bag, which will not be returned

» Fresh fruit

» Nuts

» Beef jerky

» Energy bars

» Gift card to a local restaurant

» Store-bought baked goods (many stations can't accept home-cooked items)

» Paper and craft supplies to make cards or letters

» Printed and folded gospel tract from the following website: www.servingtogether.org/printables

» Information about your church, including service times and locations or printed "Serve Anywhere" cards from our website

Younger children can print a coloring sheet from the website.

Let's Serve:

Talk with your children about first responders and the role they play during an emergency. Explain that these men and women often risk their own safety to protect and help others and share the importance of praying regularly for them.

Whenever you and your family see an emergency vehicle on the side of the road or driving past, be intentional and take a moment to pray for the person needing help and also for the law enforcement, firefighters, and paramedics. You can pray for their safety, for wisdom to do their job well, and ultimately for their relationship with Jesus Christ.

Have your children neatly arrange the goodies into the basket or bag. You can also make cards, write letters, or color printable worksheets to express your thankfulness for our first responders. Make sure to include the printable gospel tract and information inviting them to your church within the basket or bag with your cards.

Once you are finished, visit a local police or fire station as a family to deliver your gifts. This is a simple way to help children develop positive relationships with these community helpers. In rare cases, some policies prevent emergency responders from accepting gifts. If this happens, you can still give them the cards or letters and simply bless someone else with the goodies you've gathered.

Let's Pray:
Father God, we thank You so much for the men and women all around us who are willing to risk their lives daily to keep us and our family safe. We pray that You would bless them with safety while they carry out their daily jobs. We pray that you would bless them with wisdom to do their job well. We ask Lord that if they don't know You that they would

come to know and love You as their Savior and Lord. In the name of Jesus, we pray. Amen.

Let's Reflect:

23

Caring for God's Creation

"The Lord God took the man and put him in the garden of Eden to work it and keep it." Genesis 2:15

Let's Talk:

Children love nature, and most jump at the opportunity to be outside. This week, let's talk with them about making a connection between their love for nature and an understanding of their responsibility to care for this gift.

"In the beginning, God created the heavens and the earth." (Genesis 1:1)

God created the world, and we are intended to be good stewards. By teaching your children that the earth is a gift from God, you can help them understand how to better care for and wisely use its resources. Teaching your children to be good stewards is another way to honor God as a family by honoring His creation.

Let's Prep:

You will need the following:

- » Disposable gloves (for adults and children)

- » Trash bags

Pick a local park, beach, or public area that needs a little TLC. You may want to contact the local authorities responsible for overseeing the area to let them know of your clean-up plans.

You can also recruit others to help with this service project. Cleaning with others always seems to be more fun and productive.

Let's Serve:

Talk with your children about why it's important to take care of the world God has entrusted to our care. Ask them to come up with small ways to make a difference as a family (i.e., conserve water while brushing their teeth, turn off the lights when leaving the room, recycle, or maybe start a small garden).

Next, visit the area you will be cleaning and discuss some basic safely rules (i.e., children should not pick up anything sharp!). While serving, help little ones pick up larger, easier items like empty water or soda bottles. Older children can help pick up paper trash and smaller items. You may find it encouraging to take a before-and-after picture of the area to see the difference a little cleaning can make.

When you are finished, take some time to enjoy the newly cleaned area. Play ball or Frisbee and just enjoy playing in the area together. Chat with your children about God's amazing creation and be sure to thank God for it!

Let's Pray:

Dearest God, we thank You today for Your awesome creation, nature! May we appreciate and enjoy its beauty and do our part in caring for it. Help us to learn new ways to make a difference with our goal being to bring You glory. In the name of Jesus, we pray. Amen.

Let's Reflect:

24

Serving Through Foster Care and Adoption

"Religion that is pure and undefiled before God the Father is this: to visit orphans and widows in their affliction, and to keep oneself unstained from the world." **James 1:27**

Let's Talk:

When I was a child, I watched a video about an orphanage in China. Ever since that day, my heart has desired to make an impact in the lives of children through adoption. As Christians, we know God's heart is for adoption because He has adopted us into His forever family (Ephesians 1:5).

When a Christian adopts a child, it is a beautiful reflection of God's heart for adoption on display in our lives. Whether through foster care or adoption, these children need us, the church, to step up and ask God to show us how we can change our lives for their sake. Why? They are worth it! Let's talk with our children about how these children are image-bearers like you and me.

Let's Prep:

When considering adoption or foster care, research the requirements in your area. It can be helpful to talk with other foster or adoptive parents or even a church support group. If you feel you have room in your heart and home, take it to the next step and serve through foster care or adoption!

Not every family is being called by God to adopt or become a foster family, but He is calling everyone to do something. There are lots of options to serve this week. Read the "Let's Serve" section to find the items you will need now and in the future.

Let's Serve:

Talk with your children about what it could look like to become a foster or adoptive family. If you have family or friends already serving in this way, talk with them and ask lots of questions. As a family, pray about how God might use your family to become involved with foster care and adoption and decide on what next steps could be for serving.

If you decide to pursue foster care, you may want to attend a foster care orientation through your local county or city department of social services. If you feel led to adopt, a simple Internet search will provide you with organizations who would love to help answer your questions and get you started.

If you are ready to serve adoptive or foster families, here are some tangible ways to love and support them:

Give items: With foster care, children can arrive at a home any time of day or night with little to no personal belongings. Many times, the foster family has only a couple of hours to prepare. If you know a family with a new placement, find out which items remain on their list of needs. Another option is to donate items to a local agency; these items will then be distributed to foster families.

Bring food: Meals can be a great help to foster and adoptive families. Whether it's a home-cooked meal, delivery, or gift cards, it makes a huge difference when someone helps out by providing meals. It is so nice to have one less thing to worry about while adjusting to a new situation.

Childcare: All parents need a break, including foster and adoptive parents! Check with the family you intend to bless to find out the specifics.

Run errands: It takes time and planning to run errands. While you are out doing errands, offer to pick up items for a foster or adoptive family. If time is an issue, many grocery stores and online retailers offer home delivery options; you can address the order so that it goes directly to the foster or adoptive family's door.

Help with daily chores: Whether it's mowing the lawn, folding laundry, or washing some dishes, offering to help with chores can be an amazing blessing.

Prayer: Pray regularly for families who have opened their home and hearts to love like Christ. Pray for abused and neglected children as they adjust to a new home and family. Pray for strength and wisdom for all involved. Pray for their future!

Include ALL children: Whether it's a birthday party, a play date, or simply a time of giving gifts, remember to include *all* children in a home. Biological, foster, adoptive, and even children in respite care deserve to be included and treated with love.

If you know a family who regularly has additional children, you may want to check with them before the holidays and plan accordingly. Your efforts will be noticed and greatly appreciated! Excluding certain children not only impacts those children; it also impacts the entire family.

Let's Pray:
Father God, each of us has a role to play in the lives of vulnerable children. Help us to know how our family can serve these children and serve the families already serving through foster care and adoption. We want to be used by You to make a lasting difference in the lives of these children. Lead us all by Your Holy Spirit. In the name of Jesus, we pray. Amen.

Let's Reflect:

25

Adopt a Family for a Holiday

"And let us consider how to stir up one another to love and good works," Hebrews 10:24

Let's Talk:

For many families reading this book, spoiling our children during the holidays is a pleasure. Every parent loves giving their children gifts, and it may be hard to imagine that thousands of families around the country live below the poverty line. As much as these impoverished parents long to bless their children in a tangible way, they simply cannot afford to purchase gifts.

This week, let's talk with our children about how to prayerfully consider serving less fortunate families during a holiday this year.

Let's Prep:

Using your current financial situation, determine which holiday would work best for your family to bless another family. If you can afford to give generously in December, you should consider choosing Christmas. If Christmas isn't right for your family financially, you can choose a different holiday, such as

Valentine's Day. The focus of this service project is giving; don't get hung up on choosing the holiday.

Find a family to bless. If you already know a family struggling financially, this may take only a little effort. If you don't have a family in mind yet, talk to a friend or maybe your church or school for an idea of who you could bless.

Items:

The gifts you buy and the amount you spend will depend on your choice of the holiday and your current financial situation. These decisions may be best made before involving the children, who would no doubt have plenty of ideas on how best to spend your money. You may want to see if another family or families would like to join you and purchase gifts, as well. Many hands make light work. Buying the items together will be a part of the service project, so don't purchase the items in advance.

Contact the family being blessed in advance. Let them know what you have in mind and keep the conversation short to prevent any potential embarrassment to the family. If you know the family and feel that it may be awkward for them, you may want to take a different approach, such as leaving the gift(s) at the front door a couple days before the holiday and taking the "ding, dong, ditch" approach.

Let's Serve:

Now that you have a budget and you've picked a holiday and a family, it's time to serve with your children. Start by explaining how blessed your family is and how fortunate they are to receive gifts. Depending upon the age of your child and whether you know the family you are blessing, you may want to go a little more in-depth into the topic of poverty. If you know the family, it is likely best to keep it simple, as children are great at repeating things they hear. Unintentionally, an innocent conversation could have a negative impact if your children speak with the children in the other families.

Encourage your children to help pick out the gifts. Whether it's in the store or online, they will love picking out items for the other family. If your children are older, you may want to see if they want to help pay for some of the items with their own money or money they earn by doing some extra chores. You might be surprised by what your children are willing and even eager to give.

If your children are reluctant, it is best not to force them to use their money. A giving heart is not made by force. If you feel giving is a problem for your child, pray and continue to serve because more is caught than taught. Keep in mind, heart change doesn't typically happen overnight, and changing our child's heart is ultimately the work of God.

Before delivering the gifts, be sure to pray for the family and for God's continued blessing and provision for them. Lastly, deliver the gifts.

Let's Pray:

Dearest God, thank You for our many blessings. Help us to never take our blessings for granted. May we always remember that our blessings come from You. Thank You for the opportunity to bless others. May they truly feel loved and may they give You all the credit. As our families continue serving with our children and demonstrating Your love through our actions, we ask You to mold each child's heart to be more and more considerate of the needs of others. In the name of Jesus, we pray. Amen.

Let's Reflect:

26

Busy Bags

> *"A new commandment I give to you, that you love one another: just as I have loved you, you also are to love one another. By this all people will know that you are my disciples, if you have love for one another."* **John 13:34-35**

Let's Talk:

It is usually easy to feel compassion for people suffering from poverty or sickness. We are typically moved and desire to help in some way. Sometimes, though, showing concern and empathy might not even cross our minds. Picture a child having a total meltdown while they are in the store or waiting in a long line. Unless we have been in that situation ourselves, it is far too easy to be judgmental and let our thoughts run wild.

"Why doesn't the mom do something? Why didn't this mom plan ahead and bring a toy or a snack? If that was my kid, ..." Whether we quietly remark on the situation under our breath or simply roll our eyes, our children, and others for that matter, are noticing our reaction and forming an opinion, too.

This week, let's talk with our children about ways to love others instead of ignoring them or being judgmental. We will do this all while teaching our children to see opportunities to serve others.

Let's Prep:
Before the event, collect the following items. These are only suggested items, so feel free to be creative.

- » Quart or gallon-size bag

- » Small coloring book or printable coloring sheet from our website

- » Crayons

- » Stickers

- » Play-Doh

- » Game

- » Unisex toy

- » Applesauce

- » Fig bar

- » Printed and folded tract from the following website: www.servingtogether.org/printables

- » Information about your church, including service times and locations or printed "Serve Anywhere" cards from our website.

Let's Serve:
Start by talking to your children about the meaning of compassion. Ask them for examples of how we can show compassion to others, maybe even to a parent who is having a hard day. Now you will have the opportunity to tangibly help that mom or dad by preparing a busy bag.

A busy bag is a care package designed to keep a child occupied. These bags can be kept in your car and carried with you when your family goes to a doctor's appointment, out to dinner, or to a store. Then, you will just wait for an opportunity to show kindness to someone likely having a rough day.

Arrange the items neatly in the bag, making sure not to put too much stuff in the bag or you may not be as inclined to bring it with you. When putting in your church information and the gospel tract, it is best to place these items in the back of the bag so the other items can be clearly seen. The bag should look more like a gift than something you're trying to sell.

Your children may want to include a hand-made card or a letter, letting the person know that you're praying for them. Pray with your children for the family receiving the bag and wait with anticipation for the opportunity to bless another family.

Let's Pray:
Oh Lord, thank You for the example You have set for us to love one another. We ask for the opportunity to show compassion

and love to someone soon. May You receive all the glory. In the name of Jesus, we pray. Amen.

Let's Reflect:

27

Sponsor a Child

"And he took a child and put him in the midst of them, and taking him in his arms, he said to them, 'Whoever receives one such child in my name receives me, and whoever receives me, receives not me but him who sent me.'" **Mark 9:36-37**

Let's Talk:

Child sponsorship programs are an amazing way to make a global impact as a family for less than $40 a month. The children being sponsored receive life-changing benefits, such as the ability to attend or remain in school, medical care, nutritious food, life skills and job training, and most importantly, an opportunity to hear the gospel.

When sponsoring a child, your family will have a personal connection with the child through cards, letters, and photos, as well as regular updates from the sponsorship program. In addition to helping provide for the needs of each sponsored child, these sponsorship programs also provide opportunities to personally connect with the child's family and community. When you sponsor a child, you get to see the transformation in a child's life, as lasting solutions are developed to fight poverty and enable vulnerable children to reach their God-given potential.

There are many child sponsorship organizations, but I have provided three Christ-centered, humanitarian organizations and their mission statements for your family to consider.

Compassion International

"Releasing children from poverty in Jesus' name is a mission about love. We love God, and we demonstrate our love and live out our faith by extending care to others and living out the meaning of compassion."

Christian Relief Fund

"Christian Relief Fund is dedicated to the poverty ridden children's growth intellectually, physically, spiritually, and socially. In order to stay focused on their mission, CRF follows these four core values: Caring for Children, Committed to Christ, Working through Churches, and Operating with Authenticity."

World Vision

"World Vision is an international partnership of Christians whose mission is to follow our Lord and Savior Jesus Christ in working with the poor and oppressed to promote human transformation, seek justice, and bear witness to the good news of the Kingdom of God."

This week, let's talk with our children about child sponsorship as a family and consider sponsoring a child.

Let's Prep:

Take some time to prayerfully consider if sponsoring a child is right for you and your family. If you decide to sponsor a child, set aside some time to pick the organization most closely aligned with your values and goals for child sponsorship. After praying, if you decide that this is not currently a good fit or not financially feasible, you may want to prayerfully consider making a one-time donation to one of the above organizations or any Christ-centered humanitarian organization.

If you decide to proceed with sponsoring a child, prayerfully pick a child to sponsor. Most organizations provide the ability for you to search for a child to sponsor by using a birth date, age, gender, or location. This can foster a more personal connection to the child being sponsored.

Feel free to include your children during this part of the preparation. Keep in mind that some children may feel overwhelmed by the number of children in need, so some families choose to exclude younger children from this part of the child sponsorship process.

When your child sponsorship informational packet arrives in the mail, you can begin the "Let's Serve" section.

Let's Serve:

Start this service project by discussing world poverty with your children. Some facts may be difficult for children to understand, but remember that the goal is to stir in them a desire to serve others in need. An easy way to begin is by sharing some facts about poverty, including:

» Globally, more than 10 percent of the population lives on less than $2 a day

» More than 60 million children are not attending school

» Billions of people worldwide lack access to clean water

Next, talk with your children about the organization your family has chosen and share how the goal is to make an impact on the world's most poverty-stricken areas in the name of Jesus. As a family, read over the informational packet about your family's child sponsorship and pray together for the sponsored child. Invite your children to write cards or letters of encouragement; they can also draw pictures to send to the sponsored child.

If you already sponsor a child, great! You can use this opportunity to pray for the sponsored child and have your children send cards or letters.

Let's Pray:

Father God, we thank You for amazing Christ-centered organizations and how they are using their time and resources to make a positive impact on global poverty and an eternal impact on the lives of those being served. Thank You for the opportunity to take part in this important work. May this service project help our children develop an enduring compassion for others in need. In the name of Jesus, we pray. Amen.

Let's Reflect:

28

The Persecuted Church

"Remember those who are in prison, as though in prison with them, and those who are mistreated, since you also are in the body." **Hebrews 13:3**

Let's Talk:

Open Doors is a nonprofit community of Christians who come together to support persecuted believers worldwide. Present in more than 70 countries, Open Doors takes time getting to know the persecuted believers on the ground. Working with local partners, they distribute Bibles and Christian literature and give discipleship training and emergency relief aid when needed.

"At Open Doors, we've made a commitment to stand with the persecuted — so they can be the light of Christ to their communities." (www.opendoorsusa.org)

Worldwide, Christians are one of the most persecuted religious groups. It is estimated that more than 200 million Christians are persecuted for their faith. This persecution comes in many forms, such as being threatened, isolated, ostracized, harassed, losing their home and assets, physically tortured, raped, imprisoned, and sometimes even killed for following Christ. The most important thing we can do for our persecuted brothers and sisters in the faith is pray.

This week, let's talk with our children about how we can spend time in prayer for the persecuted church and encourage our brothers and sisters around the world.

Let's Prep:

For decades now, Open Doors has published a World Watch List. This list includes the 50 most persecuted countries for Christians and information on the type of persecution these brothers and sisters are facing. This list can be viewed online at their website: www.opendoorsusa.org/christian-persecution/world-watch-list. You can also sign up to receive emails or download their mobile app to stay updated concerning persecuted Christians worldwide.

Pick a country to discuss with your children. Then, review the current persecution situation for that country. Be sure to pick a country experiencing persecution that you feel comfortable sharing with your children.

Let's Serve:

Start this project by talking about the enormous blessing it is for your family to freely worship God in this country. Then, explain persecution and talk in an age-appropriate way about what this means for the country you selected for family prayer. Pray together for those being persecuted. Hopefully, this service project will encourage your children to continue praying for our persecuted brothers and sisters around the world on an ongoing basis.

Next, write a message, letting persecuted brothers and sisters know that your family is praying for them. Allow your children to help decide what to include in this uplifting and encouraging message. Open Doors has an online form for messages like yours. After you've submitted the message, Open Doors shares your message to help encourage those being persecuted and remind them that they are not alone.

Lastly, prayerfully consider making a one-time or recurring donation to the amazing work being done through Open Doors.

Let's Pray:
Father God, please comfort and sustain our persecuted brothers and sisters around the world. Please bless them with strength and peace. Please allow their light to shine in such a way to cause many people to come to a saving faith in Christ Jesus. In the name of Jesus, we pray. Amen.

Let's Reflect:

29

Modern Day Slavery Awareness

> *"Rescue the weak and the needy; deliver them from the hand of the wicked."* **Psalm 82:4**

Let's Talk:

Many people believe slavery ended in the 19th century after the Emancipation Proclamation. Unfortunately, slavery still exists today in many forms. One misconception is that slavery only affects third-world countries. However, there are several forms of modern-day slavery, which continue to exist and affect every country.

For this service project, let's talk with our children about one of the most common forms of modern-day slavery: forced labor, specifically in the supply chain. Many products purchased and consumed on a regular basis are made by people in slavery. From producing, manufacturing, distributing, and retailing, products go through many phases before reaching us, the consumers.

"You might not think you have much of a personal connection to human trafficking, but if you are a believer, be reminded that you were a slave. Jesus redeemed you from that slave master called sin. And He has given us freedom. Therefore, as freed slaves, we should have a heart for those who continue in bondage—whether spiritual or physical, and in many cases, it's both. It should be our desire to continue in the path that Jesus set out for us in His earthly ministry: to proclaim good news to the poor, to proclaim liberty to the captives, to set at liberty those who are oppressed (Luke 4:18)." (Five Ways to Fight Modern-Day Slavery by Ben Reaoch)

For this service project, we will use our power as consumers to spend our money in a way more deliberately reflecting ethical choices to make a small, but meaningful difference in the fight to end modern-day slavery.

Let's Prep:
Create a list of things you intend to purchase within the next week, including clothing, snack foods, etc. Be sure to write down the brands you typically purchase.

Let's Serve:
Have an age-appropriate discussion with your children about modern-day slavery. For very small children, it can be difficult to determine what will be understood and what won't. It's never too soon to start having these discussions as we strive to develop a Christ-honoring perspective of justice and a lifelong heart for service.

Next, pick a few products from your list and research those products. Many companies have a Code of Conduct available for their customers to read on their website, and you can typically find a company's standards on human rights. Alternatively, it could be located on other landing pages, such as "home," "about us," "frequently asked questions," or "helpful links."

If a company is striving to make the rights of workers a priority, it is beneficial to clearly communicate such priorities to consumers through easily accessible information on their website. When organizations are being transparent about their standards on human rights, this is often a good sign.

One easy way to make your dollars count is to consider purchasing products from B-corporation organizations or products with a fair trade certification. These designations indicate a higher degree of accountability to ensure fair wages, ethical work conditions, and responsible environmental stewardship. If the brand you are researching doesn't clearly indicate the original source of their products, this could be a red flag.

Unfortunately, many companies neither have an effective policy on ethically sourcing their materials nor a way to ensure ethical supply chain accountability. Without such policies in place, a company might have a product with a lower price, but any savings realized is being made on the backs of those in modern-day slavery. When doing this service project with older children and teenagers, help them investigate the situation as if they were a detective, allowing them to do some of the research themselves.

Next, go shopping. Whether it's online or at the grocery store, spend each dollar this week to support products offered by companies and brands working towards ending modern-day slavery. This service project can be simple or extremely complex. It just depends on your comfort level for yourself and your family. Even if it's only going to the store to buy a fair trade candy bar, you can still use that as an opportunity to explain the impact a purchase can make.

Then, tell others about what you learned! One of the most powerful ways to fight slavery is to spread the word. Choose at least two people to tell what you learned this week. You might even consider telling friends and family about a new favorite ethically sourced brand you discovered. When sharing why you now care about this issue, you will have opportunities to clearly point to the gospel and the hope found in Christ Jesus alone.

Lastly, as we pray, let's keep in mind to not only pray for those currently in slavery, but also for their oppressors.

"But an amazing thing about the Gospel of Jesus is that it's a message not only for the oppressed, but also for the oppressors; not only to the victim, but to the perpetrators. Remember, 'Love your enemies...' The good news of Jesus crucified for sinners and victorious over death is a message of hope for both the slave and the human trafficker...The gospel is a message of hope for all who will repent and believe." (Five Ways to Fight Modern-Day Slavery by Ben Reaoch)

Let's Pray:

Father God, may the focus of this service project and all projects be the gospel. Help each of us remember that we were once slaves to sin and have now been freed by the precious blood of Christ Jesus. We pray for those who live in physical and spiritual slavery. We ask for their freedom and for a peace that can only be found through a relationship with Jesus. We also pray for the oppressors to be captured and prosecuted, but most importantly to come to a saving faith though Jesus Christ. Lead us Lord as we lead our children in the way that they should go. In the name of Jesus, we pray. Amen.

Let's Reflect:

30

Clean Water

Let's Talk:

Most of us have never considered how blessed we are to have clean, safe water. Hundreds of millions of people in developing countries throughout the world are not so fortunate. Every day, they live without access to clean, safe water and basic sanitation. For drinking water, some obtain water from ponds, rivers, and swamps, subjecting themselves and their families to many waterborne illnesses.

In Africa and Asia, typically women and children carry the burden of walking an average of 3.7 miles per day, hauling more than 40 pounds of water to their homes. This great responsibility takes time and energy away from being able to do other things, including working a job or even attending school.

Lifewater International is a Christian nonprofit organization whose mission is to end the global water and sanitation crisis, one village at a time. Their unique set-up offers your family the chance to choose a water project, and their website (www.lifewater.org) allows you to see how many families will be positively impacted by the clean water. You can even see pictures and read testimonials from some of those families. As a project is funded, you can follow periodic updates, sharing the details associated with every major step to project completion.

For this week's service project, let's talk with our children about a unique way to get involved in helping to end the world's water crisis. By now, I'm sure everyone has heard of people donating their birthdays to a cause. From the youngest to the oldest, everyone has a birthday and can turn a special day into a life-changing day, blessing others as we have been richly blessed.

Let's Prep:
Decide ahead of time what you feel will work best for your family. Feel free to start small. If your child has not heard of someone donating their birthday before, I would suggest having one or both parents donate their birthday to set an example.

Your child will see your excitement and be able to follow along through the journey as funds are gathered and updates on your chosen project are received. Having seen one or both parents give a birthday away, your children can more easily determine their interest in doing the same for their birthday.

138

Pick a day! It doesn't need to be a birthday donated. You can pick any special day.

Let's Serve:
A few weeks before your chosen day, set up a fundraising page by visiting the following website: give.lifewater.org/takeaction. Once your website is up and running, spread the word; friends and family might be interested in participating. Be sure to share your water project's progress with others and thank those involved!

When doing this with your child, they may express mixed feelings about giving away their birthday. If so, you can allow your child to do both by celebrating in a traditional way, receiving birthday gifts and money, and designating a percentage or all of the birthday money to be donated to a Lifewater project. If that is still a bit overwhelming, your children might consider multiplying one dollar by their birthday age to donate from their birthday funds. Every little bit makes a difference!

When determining how much to give, the important thing is for your child's heart to be on board. As time goes on, continue tracking the status of the Lifewater project. After you begin to experience the joy of giving away a birthday, it might be hard to go back to traditional birthday celebrations, having seen the impact your birthday has made in the lives of others!

Let's Pray:

Lord, we praise You for the blessing of clean, safe water. Help us not to take it for granted. Lord, help us experience the joy of making an impact for You through Lifewater International in the lives of people without access to clean water. Please, use their ministry to spread the gospel and clean water throughout the developing world. Bless and protect them indeed! In the name of Jesus, we pray. Amen.

Let's Reflect:

31

Serving Through Our Talents

"As each has received a gift, use it to serve one another, as good stewards of God's varied grace." **1 Peter 4:10**

Let's Talk:

God has given each one of us, including our children, unique abilities, talents, and gifts. These are not merely for us, but to use to bless others and further His kingdom. Let's talk with our children about ways to use their talents and God-given abilities to reach those who do not know Him, giving God all the glory.

A few years ago, two sisters in Virginia started the Believers of Christ (BOC) club. These girls enjoy arts and crafts and used their talents to knit, crochet, and make different crafts to sell. They use the money that they raise to purchase Bibles.

"We wanted to use our hands to make products to glorify God, and to share the Good News of Salvation by giving Bibles away," said the founders. All the money raised by these young ladies goes directly to purchasing Bibles to give away. This week, our children will have the opportunity to "join" their club by using their God-given talents and abilities for God's glory, sharing God's Word by raising money to purchase Bibles.

Let's Prep:
For this service project, you will need to use a little creativity on how your children's talents can be used to raise funds. If they like making things like crafts or baked goods, these are easy ways to make things to sell for donations. If your child enjoys singing or maybe jumping rope, family members and friends could sponsor them to perform a mini-concert in the living room or based on successfully completing a certain number of consecutive jumps with their jump rope. Don't worry, with a little creativity, you will have an idea to discuss with your children.

Let's Serve:
Talk with your children about any talents, God-given abilities, and gifts you see in them. Explain that these talents are gifts from God and should be used for not only their enjoyment but to bring Him glory! With excitement, explain the BOC club to your children, share your vision for this service project, and let them know that all proceeds from the fundraiser will go to purchase Bibles. An even more exciting part is that your family will have the opportunity to distribute God's Word.

If your child seems less enthusiastic or even hesitant, don't worry! God has also given *you* gifts! Allow your children to see you use your gifts this week in a way to bless others. Point out examples of others using their God-given talents to serve others. Then, revisit this service project in a few weeks.

If your children are excited and ready to join the BOC club, move along with your planned fundraiser. Once your family has raised the funds, it's time for a trip to the store to pick out and purchase the Bibles. Your child may even want to be the one to pay the cashier.

Prayerfully consider where you will distribute the Bibles. You may choose to bless the homeless, a family shelter, or maybe you know someone who doesn't have one. Once you have distributed the Bibles, let the BOC club know, as they have a goal of distributing 1 million Bibles. As of May 2019, they were at 2,000! Way to go, girls!

BOC Club Information:
Website: https://bocclub15.wixsite.com/believersofchrist
Email: bocclub15@gmail.com

Let's Pray:
Father God, we thank You for each of our unique talents and abilities! We pray we would learn to use these gifts not merely for our own gain but also to glorify You. We ask You to use these Bibles to lead many recipients to a saving faith in You. Please bless the BOC club and help them reach their goal of distributing 1 million Bibles. We ask all of this in the name of Jesus and for His glory! Amen.

Let's Reflect:

32

Food Pantry/Bank Collection

"Jesus said to them, 'I am the bread of life; whoever comes to me shall not hunger, and whoever believes in me shall never thirst.'" **John 6:35**

Let's Talk:

When we hear the word "hunger," we often think globally, not locally. Yet, 1 of every 6 people in the United States (more than 41 million) face hunger. In this country, hunger is not the result of a food supply shortage. In fact, approximately 40 percent of the food in the US is thrown away each year.

The cause of hunger in the US is attributed to those living below the poverty level. With that many Americans struggling to feed their families, people are relying on food banks and church pantries to help meet the overwhelming need. This week, let's talk with our children about this need in our local community, which should compel us to act.

Let's Prep:

Before collecting items, find the best place to drop off food donations and identify the items currently needed at the facility. The best place to start is your church. If they have a food pantry, find out what they need or are currently collecting. If you are not connected to a food pantry through your church, you will need to do a bit of work. Make sure the organization you decide to support is not merely providing food, but also sharing the gospel.

> *"It is so important that nourishment is spiritual as well as physical. If the Gospel is not being shared along with the distribution of food, then only physical hunger is relieved. The spiritual hunger still aches inside." - Fulfilling More Than Physical Needs by Rebekah Jacobson*

Let's Serve:

Spend time discussing age-appropriate facts about US hunger with your children. With your children, review the list of items needed at the local food bank or church pantry and allow them to come up with of ways to collect these items. They could check the cabinets or ask family members or friends. Feel free to simply make a grocery run with your children to get the items.

Once all the nonperishable items have been collected, spend some time praying for those receiving the items. Talk about the importance of feeding a person spiritually, as well as physically. Lastly, have your children come with you, if possible, to drop off the items collected for donation.

Let's Pray:

Lord, we thank You for the opportunity to give tangible help to others. May the people receiving these donations not only be fed physically but most importantly spiritually. John 6:35 says, "I am the bread of life; whoever comes to me shall not hunger, and whoever believes in me shall never thirst. May they come to know and love You as their Savior and Lord. In the name of Jesus, we pray. Amen.

Let's Reflect:

33

Showing Hospitality

"Above all, keep loving one another earnestly, since love covers a multitude of sins. Show hospitality to one another without grumbling." **1 Peter 4:8-9**

Let's Talk:

When I was a new mom, I remember how stressed I was every time someone said they were going to visit. I truly believed everyone had their act together except me. As I would run around the house quickly putting away toys and trying to fold the pile of laundry that had likely been on my couch for days or weeks, it would take the joy out of having visitors.

When a guest would come by unexpectedly, I would — and still do —spend the first 5 to 10 minutes apologizing for every item that wasn't in its place and warning them to use the bathroom at their own risk. The truth is none of my friends wanted to come over and see a spotless house; they wanted to spend time with me and my family. Many moms are relieved to see that their friends don't have it all together either.

The problem with this attitude is that our children grow up seeing us panic when a guest is coming instead of seeing our heart for hospitality. Our home should be a welcoming environment for everyone. Of course, we all want things to be in order, but many times it's just not practical. Instead, let's set a different example for our children and talk with them about welcoming guests with calm and cheerful hearts.

Let's Prep:
No preparation is required.

If you would like to have some fun cleaning up around the house, play 15 minutes of clean-up tunes. For suggestions, visit the following website: www.servingtogether.org/resourse

Let's Serve:
Most of our children have some sort of responsibility when it comes to cleaning the house. Before bed or before leaving the house, you may want to add a 15-minute clean-up session, which helps children learn to put things back in their place. You may need to walk through a task with your child a few times, but even my 1 and a half year old can throw dirty clothes in the laundry if specifically instructed.

When a friend calls last minute or shows up on your doorstep, you may be tempted to run around like crazy. Remember that you're just living life, and sometimes life is messy. You have times when your family cleans up, and you have times to enjoy having company. Allow your children to see hospitality as being more important than a spotless home. Instead of the mad dash with you and your children trying to hide every mess before your company arrives, discuss things your children can do to be hospitable. Remember, hospitality is about loving others; it's more than a clean home.

Here are a few ideas to be more hospitable:

» Welcome your guest inside with a smile

» Offer to take and hang up coats and other belongings

» Offer your guest a drink

» If your guest has children, your children (preschool and up) could let their friends pick the activity

» Remind your children to practice sharing, which can be very hard

» Allow your children to come up with other ideas on how to make guests feel welcome

» If you know a guest is coming, have your children help you prepare a snack that they can offer during the visit

» Thank your guest for coming and invite them to come back

"Showing hospitality is a great way to do ministry and we should remember that other women relate to our "messy house" struggles and desire a friendship, not a sparkling home to be shown to them." -**Jen, The Purposeful Mom**

Let's Pray:

Father God, we thank You for the opportunity to be hospitable to others and set an example for our children. Help us demonstrate Your love through our actions. Give us many opportunities to love others more than a clean home. In the name of Jesus, we pray. Amen.

Let's Reflect:

34

Salvation Army Kettle Bell Ringing

"Make a joyful noise to the Lord, all the earth!" **Psalm 100:1**

Let's Talk:

The Salvation Army's mission is to "preach the gospel of Jesus Christ and to meet human needs in His name without discrimination." Assisting approximately 25 million people in 130 countries, the Salvation Army provides disaster relief, emergency shelters; specific aid and programs for the needy and poor (food, financial assistance, day care, job training, etc.); youth recreation and development programs; and more.

One of the most visible ways the Salvation Army fundraises is through Kettle Bell Ringing. This fundraising method is critical to provide for the physical and spiritual programs available through the Salvation Army. The funds raised through Kettle Bell Ringing are invested back into the communities where the money was raised, helping our neighbors in times of hardship and disaster.

For this project, we will ring the bell and talk with our children about being the hands and feet of Jesus everywhere we go.

Let's Prep:
Visit the Salvation Army website and find the location closest to you. Sign up for at least a two-hour block between 10 am and 8 pm, Monday through Saturday. Kettles are located at grocery stores and retail shops in most areas.

Be sure to pack water and a snack, as well as a stroller or seats for little ones. Also, check the weather forecast and prepare accordingly. If cold weather is expected, you might consider bringing a pack of handwarmers and a warm beverage. If hot weather is expected, have a cool beverage on hand. Whatever the weather, being prepared and comfortable can help as you greet many people with a smile and a jingle.

Let's Serve:
Talk to your children about the wonderful things the Salvation Army is doing for the community and worldwide. If you see anyone ringing a kettle bell before you have signed up for a shift, encourage your children to drop a few coins in the kettle. This can help with starting or continuing the conversation with your children about the Salvation Army, while also getting them more excited about doing Kettle Bell Ringing as a family.

This service project is fairly simple for children of all ages and abilities. When your scheduled time comes, your children will simply ring a bell and smile, letting their charm do the rest.

Let's Pray:

Oh Lord, we thank You for the opportunity to support the important work being done through the Salvation Army. We ask You to continue blessing this organization as they seek to help those in need physically and spiritually. May the many people served by them come to saving faith in Jesus. Lead us, Lord, as we continue to work towards instilling a heart of service in our children. In the name of Jesus, we pray. Amen.

Let's Reflect:

35

Contact Your Representative

"Let every person be subject to the governing authorities. For there is no authority except from God, and those that exist have been instituted by God." **Romans 13:1**

Let's Talk:

Each election season, the media is full of political campaign ads. If our children aren't seeing it on TV or hearing it on the radio, they are still seeing it on bumper stickers and signs all around the community. Everyone, including children, will be impacted by decisions made by these elected officials. These elected men and women represent everyone in their jurisdiction, including children.

Though most of our children are many years away from voting, it is never too soon to start teaching them that they have a voice and should speak up for what is right. When an elected official is contacted by many people from their jurisdiction who share the same input, these voices can directly influence decisions.

For this service project, let's talk with our children about using their voice to speak up for what is right.

Let's Prep:

Pick a topic that your family is passionate about, such as life, family, religious freedom, etc. Then, review proposed legislation relating to the selected topic, which will be voted on in the future. If you need help getting started, you can visit the Family Policy Alliance website at www.familypolicyalliance. com to find additional ideas and information. Their vision is "a nation where God is honored, religious freedom flourishes, families thrive, and life is cherished." On their website, you will find out more about issues that could potentially affect your family.

Let's Serve:

Start a conversation with your children about the pending legislation that is near and dear to your family. Discuss why this specific issue matters from a biblical perspective. For younger children, keep this discussion short and to the point. Don't worry if they don't understand everything at this point because they will soon enough.

Next, write a letter to your elected official about the cause that your family has selected. For young children, allow them to color a picture to be included with your family's letter. Be sure to keep your letter respectful, positive, and to the point. Once your letter and picture are finished, you have a few delivery options.

Snail mail: When sending mail to an elected official, snail mail can take on an entirely new meaning. Due to safety measures in place to ensure nothing dangerous passes through the mail, it could potentially take weeks before a staff member receives your letter. In some cases, the pending legislation may already have been voted on for consideration.

Email: Many people choose to email their opinions rather than sending a letter through the regular mail. Emails are received by staff members whose responsibility is taking notes and tallying up opinions. These are then passed on to the elected official. If you choose this option, the letter will be received in a timely manner. Remember to scan and attach any drawings by your children in the email.

Fax: It might surprise you to know that faxing can be the most effective way to send your letter. It will be received in a timely manner and is more likely to be passed on to the elected official, instead of being merely tallied up. If you can fax your letter, this method is a great option.

Regardless of how you choose to send your letter, you and your family can be excited and grateful for the opportunity to have your voice heard. By using your voice to advocate for something important to your family, you are also setting an example for your children to follow. Even when the decisions by elected officials don't reflect our voices, we can be encouraged to know our voices are always heard by our Father in heaven. Praying for our country and the elected officials and leaders is good and pleasing to God.

Let's Pray:

Lord, thank You for always hearing us when we use our voices to pray. We pray You would help our elected officials and leaders make decisions that honor You and restrain evil and promote good. Help us remember Your authority is supreme and all authorities have been instituted by You. Lead and enable us, as we seek to raise up a generation to love You and use their voices for Your glory. We ask You to use our seemingly small voice to accomplish Your mighty purposes. We know that our little is made much in the Master's hand. In the name of Jesus, we pray. Amen.

Let's Reflect:

36

Blessing a Faraway Family Member

"We love because he first loved us." **1 John 4:19**

Let's Talk:

As we train our children to serve and love others, we can find opportunities in our own extended family. It can be difficult for us to develop and maintain meaningful relationships with extended family members, but it can create opportunities to share the gospel when we make an effort. As we love others, it is never our job to change someone's heart. We know changing hearts is something only God can do.

"And I will give them one heart, and a new spirit I will put within them. I will remove the heart of stone from their flesh and give them a heart of flesh, that they may walk in my statutes and keep my rules and obey them. And they shall be my people, and I will be their God." Ezekiel 11:19-20

It is our job to love others, share the gospel, and pray for God to change hearts through saving faith. As we love our extended family, let us pray for the Lord to use us as a light in the lives of those in our family circle. Ask God to soften the hearts of those in our extended family to the gospel.

Sometimes unforgiveness holds us back from maintaining relationships with extended family members. If you have been struggling with unforgiveness, let me encourage you to take time to forgive through your relationship with Jesus. We don't forgive others because they deserve it or ask for it. We forgive because God has forgiven us and desires for us to forgive others.

"Be kind to one another, tenderhearted, forgiving one another, as God in Christ forgave you." Ephesians 4:32

Let's Prep:
Pick a family member to love on from afar. I would suggest picking a family member you haven't seen or spoken with in a while. It could be someone whom your children have never even met. If you don't have any extended family, you might consider someone from your past to choose, such as a family friend, old neighbor, or school friend.

You will need a device to create a video recording, such as a cell phone or video camera.

Let's Serve:
First, talk with your children about why it is important to stay connected with those living far away. Then, come up with a plan to engage more regularly with those in your extended family. Next, decide where you would like to make your video

162

greeting and what you might say to your relative or friend. Your child might like talking about how they're doing in school or share about their favorite sport. Young children can do almost anything and be adorable. They could sing a song or recite a favorite Bible verse.

When making the video, try to keep it under 5 minutes and let the recipient know your family is praying for them. Pray for them before and after making the greeting and send this beautiful greeting with no strings attached.

Let's Pray:
Dearest God, please use this project to reconnect families and friends with each other. Through these connections, we pray for each of these people to come to saving faith! May those receiving these videos truly feel loved and blessed. In the name of Jesus, we pray. Amen.

Let's Reflect:

37

Pray for Unreached People Groups

> *"So faith comes from hearing, and hearing through the word of Christ."* **Romans 10:17**

Let's Talk:

Salvation from our sins, a restored relationship with God, and a place for us in heaven is obtained by grace alone, through faith alone, and in Jesus Christ alone. What about people who have never heard the Good News of what Christ has done?

For "everyone who calls on the name of the Lord will be saved." How then will they call on him in whom they have not believed? And how are they to believe in him of whom they have never heard? And how are they to hear without someone preaching? And how are they to preach unless they are sent? As it is written, 'How beautiful are the feet of those who preach the good news!'" Romans 10:13-15

As followers of Christ, God calls us to share the Good News of Jesus Christ with those who have not heard. This urgent calling is not just for some Christians; it is a commandment to every true follower of Jesus.

"And Jesus came and said to them, 'All authority in heaven and on earth has been given to me. Go therefore and make disciples of all nations, baptizing them in the name of the Father and of the Son and of the Holy Spirit, teaching them to observe all that I have commanded you. And behold, I am with you always, to the end of the age.'" Matthew 28:18-20

As we raise our children to have a servant's heart, we are raising them to be mission-minded and understand this calling on their lives. This week, let's talk with our children about some of the unreached people in the world, estimated to be approximately 3 billion people. We will be praying for the gospel to reach them!

Let's Prep:
Download the "Unreached of the Day" app or visit joshuaproject.net to find information on unreached people groups worldwide.

Let's Serve:
The Joshua Project is a research initiative that daily highlights the unreached people groups of the world. Through their "Unreached of the Day" app or their website, your family can serve by praying for missionaries to go and share the gospel, for churches to be planted, and for eternal lives to be saved.

Over the next seven days, you and your family will have the opportunity pray for the gospel to reach the ends of the earth. Each day, share the stories with your children by providing them with information and pictures. Next, pray! Whether you choose to do this in the morning or evening, be sure to set aside a time each day for the entire week to pray for the gospel to spread among the nations. In addition, use this time to pray for your children's hearts to be open to wherever God leads them to serve in the future.

Let's Pray:
We know, Lord, that You are not slow to fulfill your promises, but are patient, not wishing that any should perish, but that all should reach repentance. We ask, Lord, for You to send Your people to share Your Good News with every nation, from all tribes, peoples, and languages. May the name of Jesus Christ reach the ends of the earth. In the name of Jesus, we pray. Amen.

Let's Reflect:

38

Celebrating Life

"For You formed my inward parts; You knitted me together in my mother's womb. I praise You, for I am fearfully and wonderfully made. Wonderful are Your works; my soul knows it very well." **Psalm 139:13-14**

Let's Talk:

Our children are introduced to the topic of abortion through church sermons, highway billboards, protesters in the news, discussions with peers, and elsewhere. As parents, we need to be ready to have this discussion with our children. In today's world, it is important for us to help our children navigate this topic from a biblical worldview. Discussing the topic of adoption should be done with love and compassion for the baby and the mother.

Our nation has legalized abortion, and our society has normalized it. In the midst of this reality, we must teach our children about the One who gives life and forms us in the womb. We must educate our children on the importance of defending life at all stages. As parents, we must be diligent to train our children to know God's view on life. If we don't teach them God's view, our children's view on abortion will likely be formed by society's ungodly view.

While doing research for this service project, I decided to search this topic on the internet to see what parents are teaching their children about abortion. I was shocked to find lots of information about how to have a pro-choice conversation, but not nearly as much about the importance and value of life. One parenting site encourages parents to talk about abortion as being a "simple medical procedure or pill" and suggesting "not using the term baby, as our children will think of 'a baby in arms' and not understand."

Depending upon your child's age, prayerfully discuss with your spouse how you would like to go about addressing this topic. If you decide to not discuss abortion at this time, you can continue with the service project, which includes serving women going through a difficult time yet choosing life for their baby.

Let's Prep:
For those choosing to discuss abortion with your children, be prepared. As you discuss the importance of life at all ages with your children, it will be hard for many of them to understand why anyone would choose to end a pregnancy. It may be helpful to explain it this way to your children: Without a relationship with Christ, it is hard for a person to navigate right from wrong, following only the law of man.

Many women are being told that abortion is their legal right as women, and it is the best option if they don't feel ready to be a mother. Instead of receiving help during a difficult time, these women are often encouraged to terminate their pregnancies due to economic hardships. We must pray for the millions of women believing these lies, asking God to have compassion and reveal the truth about abortion to them.

Save the date!
Check your calendar and pick an available Saturday morning or early afternoon to host a yard sale.

Optional materials:

> » Poster board to make signage to draw attention to your sale

> » Price stickers (not required, but they are helpful)

> » Tarp, blanket, or table to lay items on

If having a yard sale seems overwhelming, you might consider selling items online.

Lastly, locate a Christian pregnancy help center in your area. When Christ is the focus of a pregnancy help center, a baby's life isn't the only life saved! Find out which items are currently needed to support the mothers at their center.

Let's Serve:

Before discussing abortion, start the conversation by talking about the importance of life and God's design. Let your children know about the local pregnancy help center and their purpose. Explain that many of the women choosing life for their babies will need a lot of help, and one way a pregnancy center typically helps is by providing material items once the baby is born.

A week or two before your yard sale, gather items around your house to sell at your yard sale. The funds from the sale will be used to purchase items needed by the pregnancy help center. Some pregnancy centers accept items such as formula and diapers, while others need things like clothes, strollers, and even cribs. As you gather things you want to sell, feel free to ask your friends and family to donate items, as well.

If you want to draw more attention to your yard sale, have your children help make a few signs to put up around the community a couple days before the event. You may even want to let others know via email or social media in case they would like to stop by the sale. After the sale is over, you may choose to donate the remaining items or save them for another sale.

With your children, select and purchase items for the pregnancy help center. Lastly, have your children come with you when delivering the items. By including your children as much as possible, you are helping develop their hearts to have compassion and serve others.

Let's Pray:

Dearest God, may we raise up a generation that knows and loves You and honors Your creation. Help us raise a generation to value life at all stages and ages. Lead us as we navigate these difficult topics in a world that is against us because it is against You. Make us to be a continuous light in this dark, fallen world, leading people to You. In the name of Jesus, we pray. Amen.

Let's Reflect:

39

Bible Distribution

"Your word is a lamp to my feet and a light to my path."
Psalm 119:105

Let's Talk:

As discussed in the previous service project about the persecuted church, we are extremely blessed to have the freedom to worship God without fear in this country. Millions of people worldwide do not have this privilege; in many countries, Bibles are illegal. These brothers and sisters in Christ long to have access to God's Word, which is something many of us can so easily take for granted. It is therefore hugely important for us to remember to praise and thank God for this privilege.

Open Doors was founded by a man known as Brother Andrew or "God's Smuggler." For decades, Brother Andrew courageously smuggled illegal Bibles to Christians who had no access to God's Word. Open Doors continues to take risks to make sure the gospel is shared with our persecuted brothers and sisters worldwide.

"We stake our lives in Jesus' Great Commission. We take this command so seriously that we still take risks to this day to get copies of the Gospel into hostile areas. We do this because we love God." – **Open Doors**

This week, let's talk with our children about helping Open Doors reach persecuted Christians in some of the most dangerous areas of the world simply by reading their Bibles!

Let's Prep:
For the service project, you will need a Bible.

Let's Serve:
Discuss with your children how great a privilege it is to be able to own and read the Bible. Tell them about how Open Doors makes it possible for people being persecuted to read the Bible and provide them with training to understand it and share Jesus with others. To help Open Doors provide God's Word, your children will serve by doing a Bible reading challenge!

The challenge is simple: You will sponsor your child to read at least one chapter a day in their Bibles for a week. For every day that your child reads at least one chapter, you will commit $1 towards purchasing a Bible for our persecuted brothers and sisters in Christ worldwide. After reading one chapter a day for only one week, your child will be able to provide one Bible to a persecuted Christian! If financially able, encourage your children to keep reading and continue earning Bibles while learning from God's Word.

For younger children who are not yet reading, you will simply read together with them. If this is your first time reading the Bible, or if it's been a while, I would suggest starting in the New Testament with the book of John. When you are done, visit www.opendoorsusa.org/bibles-and-discipleship to make your donation for Bibles.

Let's Pray:

Lord, we thank You for the privilege we have to read and study Your Word without fear of harm or persecution. Please continue to enable Open Doors to support our brothers and sisters in Christ worldwide. Protect them as they risk their safety to live out Your Great Commission. We ask that Your church would continue to grow in these persecuted areas. May the gospel continue to spread, and lives forever be changed. In the name of Jesus, we pray. Amen.

Let's Reflect:

40

Supporting AWANA Go

"Do your best to present yourself to God as one approved, a worker who has no need to be ashamed, rightly handling the word of truth." **2 Timothy 2:15**

Let's Talk:

Have you heard about Awana? The Awana program is done through local churches in all 50 states for more than 100 Christian denominations. Worldwide, Awana GO reached more than 4 million children in 120 countries. The Awana curriculums are designed to reach children (ages 2-18) and their families with the gospel. Through the Bible stories and lessons shared during large group time, and memorizing Bible verses in Awana handbooks, Awana gives children the opportunity to put their trust in Jesus Christ and disciples them to follow Him.

"Awana equips local volunteers in churches around the world with Biblical evangelism and discipleship solutions so that today's children may become tomorrow's Christian leaders, in every aspect of society and culture." - **Awana**

This week, we will have fun memorizing Scripture while talking with our children about helping the Awana program continue to live out the Great Commission.

Let's Prep:
For each child, you will need a Bible and one sponsor printout form. Print the sponsor printout from the following website: www.servingtogether.org/printables

Let's Serve:
If your children are unfamiliar with the Awana program, start by telling them about Awana's mission. Then, explain how a verse-a-thon fundraiser works.

Awana GO started this awesome fundraiser called a verse-a-thon. Each child asks their family and friends to sponsor them for reciting as many verses from memory as they can on a specific date. The funds they raise enable Awana to start new Awana clubs worldwide. For every $10 earned during a verse-a-thon, one child will have the opportunity to be discipled through an Awana club.

Help your child set a goal of how many verses they are planning to recite. You are free to ask anyone to be a sponsor. You might consider asking a neighbor, friend, or family member. This doesn't have to be a huge financial commitment on their part because any amount will help! Next, pick the date and time to recite these memorized verses.

If your child is already in Awana, find out if their group will be participating in a verse-a-thon. If so, wait and do this service project with them. Help your child make a list of verses they already know. If they've never done Scripture memory before, now is a good time to start. You can visit our website for a list of some verses to consider memorizing. These recommended verses can be found on the following www.servingtogether.org/resources

Allow your children to have at least one week to work on memorizing their Bible verses before the specified day. When the day arrives, sit down with your child and allow them to recite their memorized verses. Whether it's 1 or 21, be excited for them and praise their efforts.

Add up the number of verses recited, then contact the sponsors to let them know how many verses were recited and how much was earned based on their support pledge. Collect the pledged amount from each sponsor and send them to support Awana GO at the following website: www.awana.org/donate.

Pray for God to reach many children through the Awana GO program. Pray also for those children who will now participate in Awana because of your fundraising.

Let's Pray:
Lord, we thank You for the opportunity to be part of Awana, living out the Great Commission. We ask You to continue blessing and providing for Awana as they share the gospel with

children and make disciples worldwide for Your glory. We pray for our children to continually hide Your Word in their hearts, so that they might not sin against You. Cause Your Word to be a lamp to their feet and a light to their path. Grow in them a love for You and Your life-giving Word. In the name of Jesus, we pray. Amen.

Let's Reflect:

41

Create Back-to-School Backpack

"And the crowds asked him, 'What then shall we do?' And he answered them, 'Whoever has two tunics is to share with him who has none, and whoever has food is to do likewise.'" **Luke 3:10-11**

Let's Talk:

Millions of children in the United States start the school year unprepared, lacking the essential school supplies needed to succeed. Across the country, churches and other organizations are aware of this great need. Many host backpack drives and collections in the mid to late summer, distributing new backpacks filled with school supplies to homeless and at-risk children throughout the US.

This week, let's talk with our children about ways to meet the physical needs of children in our community by preparing and donating backpacks with school supplies. Our goal is to give them hope as they start the school year equipped to succeed, while also giving them an eternal hope through the gospel.

Let's Prep:

Before starting, check with your church to see if they host a backpack drive. If so, they will likely have a list of items and information available for your family to participate. If you do not have a church or if your church doesn't host a backpack drive, you can check with other churches in your area or use the information here to make your own. Some stores have a school supplies list for each grade.

Suggested school supplies to purchase

- » Wide-ruled loose-leaf paper

- » Wide-ruled spiral notebooks

- » Composition books

- » Glue sticks

- » White liquid glue

- » Blue or black ink ball-point pens

- » Safety scissors

- » No. 2 pencils

- » Pencil sharpener

- » Erasers

- » Pencil case

- » Two-pocket folders

» Crayons

» Washable markers

» Colored pencils

» Ruler

» Highlighters

» 3 x 5 index cards

» Regular dividers

» Facial tissues

» Hand sanitizer

» Jesus Storybook Bible

Let's Serve:

With your list in hand, allow your children to help select the backpack and supplies needed. Once home, pack the backpack(s) full of supplies. While you and your children are packing bags, talk to them about how much these items will mean to a child in need. Pray for each child receiving a donated backpack with supplies and consider including a card in the backpack to encourage each child starting the new school year.

Many churches will have an option for you to be part of the distribution process. If this is an option, I would encourage you and your family to join them. The more our children are included in the process, the greater the impact will be on developing their heart for service. Alternatively, you could contact a local family shelter to donate any backpacks you've prepared to donate.

Let's Pray:

Lord, we thank You for the opportunity to show Your love to school-age children in need within our community. We ask that each one of these children would feel Your love through these backpacks and for many to come to saving faith in Jesus. Please, use every service project to shape our children's hearts to love You and demonstrate Your love through their desire to serve others. In the name of Jesus, we pray. Amen.

Let's Reflect:

42

Who Is My Neighbor?

"But he, desiring to justify himself, said to Jesus, 'And who is my neighbor?'" Luke 10:29

Let's Talk:

Often, people think of a racist as being an extremist, such as someone engaging in hate crimes with strong feelings of superiority towards another ethnicity. While this is certainly true of some individuals, most people are completely unaware of their own prejudices towards people from different cultures. As a whole, no one is completely without some form of a racial bias.

In many cases, we tend to feel most comfortable spending time with those who are ethnically like ourselves and do little to speak out or stand up against injustice. For those who have never experienced racial discrimination, it can be difficult to understand. Listening to others is one of the best ways to learn.

"Know this, my beloved brothers: let every person be quick to hear, slow to speak, slow to anger; for the anger of man does not produce the righteousness of God." **James 1:19-20**

Let's set aside our personal preferences and open our ears, hearts, and homes to people who are different from us. In doing so, we can better love and relate to others while learning to do good, seek justice, and correct oppression.

For this service project, we will have an opportunity to spend time with people from different cultural backgrounds. Unless this topic has been discussed with your children already, there are no discussion requirements to prepare your children for this service project. The goal of this service project is to love and get to know people from different cultures, while setting an example for your children.

When my son, Michael, was 3 years old, we spent a lot of time helping an Ethiopian woman with her teenage daughter. Her daughter was at our house daily. One day, my son was having a conversation with someone and told them he had 4 sisters. I promptly inserted myself into the conversation, counting each of his sisters for him out loud and concluding it was only 3 sisters. In response, my son was now visibly upset and loudly explained that I had forgotten one — the young Ethiopian girl. As quickly as I interrupted his conversation, I recanted, telling him that he was right. My son had no concept of their differences — in fact, they didn't matter. She was and is his sister. Amazingly enough, we eventually adopted this beautiful young lady! I am so proud to be one of her two moms.

Let's Prep:
Pick a date and time for dinner and invite a family that is culturally or ethnically different from your family. This may be easy or challenging based on where you live. Regardless, ask God to provide this opportunity.

Let's Serve:
Host a family for dinner, allowing older children to help prepare the food and younger children to help set the table and make placemats. No matter their age, be sure to engage everyone in the process.

Before choosing a meal, check with the family you are hosting to inquire about any family food allergies and any other cultural or religious food restrictions. If you don't know this family's beliefs, look for opportunities to share the gospel during your time together.

The goal is to learn and grow in your cultural understanding as a result of this experience. Remember to listen more than you speak, which can be hard for some of us to do. Don't just check the box with this service project. Enjoy your evening together, and do your best to make this a way of life for your family and the generations to come.

Let's Pray:
Lord, please bless our time with this family. Help us to get to know them better. Lead us to show hospitality as we learn more

about the beautiful differences in the people around us. In the name of Jesus, we pray. Amen.

Let's Reflect:

43

Providing Backpacks for Orphans

"Whoever receives one such child in my name receives me,"
Matthew 18:5

Let's Talk:
There are millions of children around the world who are orphaned or at risk. According to the Bible, God has a heart for the orphans, and we should, too.

Orphan Outreach is a Christ-centered nonprofit organization helping orphans and at-risk children. Their mission is to glorify the Lord Jesus Christ by ministering to orphans around the world through meeting their spiritual, physical, emotional, and educational needs. Currently, they assist children in Guatemala, Honduras, India, Kenya, Latvia, Russia, Ukraine, and the United States. They have plans to continue expanding into other countries.

This week, we will purchase and fill a backpack with essential items for Orphan Outreach to distribute to vulnerable children in schools and orphanages during upcoming mission trips.

Let's Prep:

You will need to purchase the following items, preferably with your children:

- » Backpack

- » Pencils and erasers

- » Crayons or washable markers

- » Pencil case (heavy duty with zipper)

- » Colored pencils

- » Blue or black medium point pens

- » Glue sticks

- » Scissors

- » Rulers

- » Children's multivitamins

- » First aid kit

Let's Serve:

While collecting the items, you may choose to have an age-appropriate discussion with your children about orphans and at-risk children. You can explain a little bit about Orphan Outreach and their mission to help children in need. As you pack the backpack, be sure to pray for the child who will be receiving this gift. Prayer is an important part of every service project. After packing the bag, mail it to Orphan Outreach at the following address:

Orphan Outreach
2001 West Plano Parkway, Suite 3700
Plano, Texas 75075

You might consider following Orphan Outreach on Facebook or joining their bi-weekly prayer email by visiting the following website: www.servingtogether.org/orphanoutreach. As a family, continue praying for the work that Orphan Outreach is doing for children in Jesus' name!

Let's Pray:
Lord, we pray for the children receiving these bags. We ask You to protect and watch over them. We thank You for the opportunity to help demonstrate Your love by meeting a tangible need in their lives. We pray that You would use these bags to also meet their spiritual need through the gospel message shared by Orphan Outreach. May these precious children come to have a saving faith in Jesus. Bless this ministry and expand their impact as they love and care for orphans and vulnerable children worldwide for Your glory. In the name of Jesus, we pray. Amen.

Let's Reflect:

44

Love Your Neighbor

"And He said to him, 'You shall love the Lord your God with all your heart and with all your soul and with all your mind. This is the great and first commandment. And a second is like it: You shall love your neighbor as yourself.'" **Matthew 22:37-39**

Let's Talk:

Greeting new neighbors is a tradition in many cultures and is usually an appreciated gesture. It is an awesome way to begin a relationship with a neighbor on a positive note. Being in close proximity, you will likely see each other in passing regularly. If your new neighbors are just moving to the area, your family's friendliness could help them feel welcomed and more at home in the neighborhood. Let's talk with our children about welcoming neighbors and how this is a great way to be hospitable towards others.

I remember when I was 12 years old and first experienced hospitality from neighbors. We had moved to a new neighborhood and people were bringing us dinners, brownies, house plants, and more! These kind gestures made a positive impact on my life. All these years later, I am now blessed to be the neighbor welcoming new families with dinners and treats. I pray our welcoming example of kindness and hospitality will continue in the lives of our children.

Let's Prep:

Before bringing anything to your new neighbors, introduce yourself and let them know you will be bringing something over. If you happen to bump into them as they're moving in, be sure to keep it brief and just ask what day would be best to stop by. While introducing yourself, it's a good idea to check for any potential allergies or food aversions.

Decide what you would like to bring your new neighbors. You might consider freshly baked bread, a dessert, or even a simple dinner. The point is to pick something your children can help make rather than just buying a store-bought item. If you're unable to prepare something at home, I would suggest a local specialty shop or bakery, rather than a grocery store. You and your children can pick out special treats for the neighbor to enjoy.

Make sure to purchase disposable plates and containers. The goal is to bless your new neighbors — not give them dishes to worry about cleaning and returning.

Lastly, it may be helpful to share a list of local businesses you would recommend to your neighbor based on your own experiences. Of course, these days we have the internet to find businesses. Yet, many people still love to hear first-hand recommendations from other locals when picking services such as cable, trash and recycling, plumbers, lawn maintenance, etc. This list is a great place to include your favorite local restaurants, shops, babysitters, dog walkers, and most importantly your church information and service times.

Let's Serve:

As you look through the "Let's Prep" section, feel free to figure out areas where your children would enjoy helping. With your children, prepare the items to welcome your new neighbors to the neighborhood. Have your children make placemats, cards, or anything extra they would like to add. When delivering the food, be sure to allow your children to come with you. This transaction should be short and sweet to avoid imposing on your neighbors. Let them know that you are available if they need anything, and remember to share your contact information.

Let's Pray:

Lord, we thank You for our new neighbors. We pray they would feel seen and loved! Lord, as they see our love and kindness towards them, may it point directly to You. Lord, as our relationship grows with them, we pray these neighbors would come to know they can count on our family in times of need. If they don't know You, I pray they come to saving faith and know they can always count on You. Lord, help us be more than good neighbors; help us to be Godly neighbors! In the name of Jesus, we pray. Amen.

Let's Reflect:

45

Bringing Water to the Thirsty

"Whoever believes in me, as the Scripture has said, 'Out of his heart will flow rivers of living water.'" **John 7:38**

Let's Talk:
Cold water on a hot or even warm day is refreshing. People who have been outside for hours are often on the lookout for cold water. For this easy and fun service project, we will be looking for opportunities to meet this need through cold bottles of water, ultimately seeking opportunities to share the living water found through the gospel.

Let's Prep:
Gather a case of bottled water and church information cards with service times and locations. Ensure the church information is printed on card stock and is roughly the size of a business card. If your church doesn't have something like this available, feel free to make your own. You can look at examples at the following website: www.servingtogether.org/printables

If you do not have a church that you attend regularly, feel free to print out one of the Church Anywhere cards from the website provided. You will also need to print as many Living Water Cards as needed from the website. Lastly, you will need a hole punch and balloon ribbon.

Look for information about upcoming events such as a parade, neighborhood yard sale, walk or run, etc. Find an event that works for your family's schedule. If your family has time constraints for this service project, you can skip this step.

Let's Serve:

With your children, punch holes through the church information and Living Water Cards. Then, cut the balloon ribbon into several 4-inch pieces. Your school-age children can help with cutting the ribbon. Use each piece of ribbon to feed through the hole punched in the church information and a Living Water Card. Then, tie the ribbon to the top of each water bottle to secure the cards. Do not tie the ribbon too tightly or it might cause the printed information to rip and come loose from the water bottle. On the day before the event, place the water bottles in the refrigerator. If you would like to use some of the water bottles as ice packs, simply place six water bottles or so in the freezer. The frozen water bottles will work great in a cooler instead of using ice which gradually melts and can ruin the printed cards.

If you did not pick a specific event, that is perfectly fine. Just pick a really hot day and bless those you see around you with cold water. Make it fun for everyone. Think of it as a scavenger hunt for your children as you go around the neighborhood blessing the mailman, dog walkers, trash collector, construction workers, lawn care workers, etc. Anyone you see who looks hot and thirsty is a perfect candidate to receive a bottle of cool water. If people ask why your family is giving them water, you may want to simply let them know the water is intended to bless them because God tells us to love one another. After you and your children have had a blast handing out water, be sure to pray for each person who received a water bottle. Pray that the Lord would use this kind gesture and church invitation to show His love to the person receiving it.

Let's Pray:

Father God, we thank You for the opportunity to bless men, women, and children in our community. We know this refreshing water is only temporary and that You offer a living water to quench our deepest thirst. We pray these people would accept our invitation to join us and others at our church, where they will learn more about this living water through the gospel. In the name of Jesus, we pray. Amen.

Let's Reflect:

46

Inviting Neighbors to Church

"And he said to them, 'Go into all the world and proclaim the gospel to the whole creation.'" **Mark 16:15**

Let's Talk:

The most important information you could ever share with a neighbor, friend, or family member is the gospel. Jesus paid the price for their sins by dying on the cross and raising from the dead on the third day, conquering death and purchasing a place for us in heaven! Easter is a day for Christians to celebrate the resurrection of Jesus and victory over death. Celebrating the resurrection of Jesus is not the only reason people enjoy this holiday. Some celebrate by filling baskets with chocolate bunnies, decorating eggs, egg hunts, and many other ways. Fond memories and family traditions often make Easter a special day.

Easter also gives us a unique opportunity to invite unchurched and non-believing neighbors to church. Research shows that the highest online search for churches is during the week before Easter. According to a 2016 Lifeway research study, 56 percent of Americans are very or somewhat willing to receive information about a local congregation or faith community from a friend or neighbor.

When considering inviting our neighbors to church, there are often many reasons holding us back. Through this service project, my hope is to make extending the invitation a little easier through a sweet treat. God desires for us to share the gospel. Let's talk with our children about this unique opportunity to invite our neighbors on such a special day!

Let's Prep:

Before beginning, you will need a flyer or invitation from your church for the Easter service. If your church doesn't have one, feel free to make one. Remember to include the location and service times, specifically the service time you attend.

Next, you will need a sweet treat! Use this as an opportunity for your little ones to help you bake cookies or cupcakes. If time is an issue, feel free to pick up treats from your local grocery store or neighborhood bakery. Since many families deal with allergies, you could also pick up a pack of something safe for children with allergies to enjoy.

If you do not typically go to church, this is a great opportunity to begin. After looking over the local churches' doctrinal statements and picking a church location and time that works for your family, use that information when making invitations to church for your neighbors.

Let's Serve:

Part of this service project is the preparation of the treats for the neighbors. Whether store-bought or homemade, be sure to wrap them up neatly because you'll be handing these out to several different individuals. Next, gather your family and make a game plan to invite the neighbors to church. Determine which neighbors you will be visiting and who will be doing the talking in your family. Your goal is to leave each family with a sweet treat and a personal invitation to a church service, which you will also be attending.

As you hand out your goodies, be ready to answer any questions folks may have about your church, such as the denomination or childcare. Allow your children to tell them what they're most looking forward to at the upcoming church service. Maybe the church is doing a special Easter egg hunt or a puppet show. Whatever it is, have your children tell your neighbors about it. If you've never been to the church before, be sure to let the families know that you are going to this church for the first time, too, and would like for them to join your family.

If a neighbor agrees to attend church with you, be sure to make it as comfortable and non-intimidating as possible. Meet the family in the parking lot or at the front door to show them where to check in their children, the locations of the restrooms, where your family sits, and any other information that would be helpful to make this a good experience for them.

If you don't encounter a neighbor who agrees to go to church with you, remember your children are watching to see how you respond to situations. Maintain your enthusiasm and pray with your children for those not willing to accept your family's invitation to church. Let your children know that your job is not to change their hearts. Then, continue to pray for God to do the heart work, while your family continues to display Christ's love in a multitude of ways.

This is a great service project to do during other holidays, as well, such as Christmas!

Let's Pray:

Lord, we thank You for the Good News of Jesus, which we celebrate every Easter. Thank You for sending Jesus to die on the cross and raising Him from the dead to pay the penalty for our sins and purchase a place for us in heaven. We pray for the people we invite to hear this message to have receptive hearts. With great anticipation, we look forward to seeing what You will do through families seeking to live out the Great Commission. In the name of Jesus, we pray. Amen.

Let's Reflect:

47

Cancer Care Packages

"fear not, for I am with you; be not dismayed, for I am your God; I will strengthen you, I will help you, I will uphold you with my righteous right hand." **Isaiah 41:10**

Let's Talk:

In one form or another, cancer has impacted each of our lives. Many people reading this book are currently in the trenches, and others are in remission. This topic can be a hard one to navigate. My desire is to shine a light of hope to families suffering, showing them love and compassion during this difficult time.

This week, we will have the opportunity to discuss this terrible disease at an age-appropriate level with our children. Let's talk with them about a practical way to bless individuals suffering from cancer.

Let's Prep:

To begin, collect the items listed below. The quantity depends on how many people you will be blessing.

Items needed:

> » Plastic zipper bags

> » Lemon drops or gum (for the bad taste chemo can leave)

> » Hand sanitizer

> » Lotion

> » Lip balm

> » Travel toothpaste and toothbrush

> » Water bottle

> » Journal and pen

> » Print and fold Good News tract from the following website: www.servingtogether.org/printables

The items listed above were recommended through a breast cancer survivor at the following website: www.survivordiane.com.

Let's Serve:
When starting a conversation about cancer, one option is to explain to your children what cancer is. To simplify, cells are the building blocks of life, and we have trillions of them. Cells have lots of different jobs in the body like keeping us healthy. Cancer is caused when some of the cells in our body stop doing the job they're supposed to do. These rogue cells are what make someone sick with cancer.

It is a good idea to explain to your children that cancer is not like a cold and can't be caught by being around people with cancer. We should also remind our children and ourselves that God is still in control even during the storms of cancer.

For this service project, you will be making "chemo care kits" to bless individuals starting chemotherapy. To start, talk to your children about the items being put into each bag, letting them know why the items will be helpful to someone going through chemotherapy. Regardless of your child's age, anyone can help make a care package!

Allow your children to take the items discussed and put them neatly into the bags, including an encouraging letter to let the chemo patient know you are praying for them. Many of the service projects in this book include writing letters or drawing pictures. I believe these personal letters and cards can add a meaningful touch to everything we do. If you know individuals personally going through chemotherapy, feel free to personalize the letter or card, making a bag specifically for them.

After making the bags and praying for the person in need of healing and hope, please drop your bags off at a local oncology office. Let the office know the purpose of the bags and leave them there to be a distributed. Continue to pray with your family for the individuals receiving the bags.

Let's Pray:

Father God, we thank You for the opportunity to love these individuals who will receive these care packages. We pray for You to bless them with a peace, which can only come from You during this time of storms. We ask for their complete healing and restoration, and more importantly for them to come to a saving faith in Jesus. Be glorified in the lives of these people through these bags. In the name of Jesus, we pray. Amen.

Let's Reflect:

48

Disabilities

So God created man in his own image, in the image of God he created him; male and female he created them. **Genesis 1:27**

Let's Talk:
Children are curious about the world around them. It is easy for us to become uncomfortable when that curiosity leads to questions about individuals with disabilities. This week, we will discuss a few helpful tips on navigating this topic. We will also have some fun with art while talking with our children about supporting families who have children with disabilities.

Here are a few things to keep in mind when discussing disabilities with your children:

People with special needs are different, but that's not a bad thing.
Help your children focus less on the differences and more on the things in common, such as hair, eyes, or maybe a laugh or smile. Remind your child that God made all people in his image, meaning these children are His masterpieces.

Lead by example.

Our children pick up so much from us through our words and actions. If we feel uncomfortable around people with disabilities, our children will notice and form their own conclusions, potentially causing them to avoid people with disabilities altogether. For those of us who have never experienced a child with disabilities first-hand, it can be hard for us to know how to respond. Let's start by educating ourselves. The more we know about a disability, the more our comfort level will increase.

Avoid using words like "sick."

By using such words, you can easily confuse children, as a disability is not something children will catch from someone else. As we approach this topic with compassion, we should do our best to explain what the disability is called, such as Down syndrome, autism, or cerebral palsy. Our children are smarter than we think; don't be afraid to use "big" words.

It would be a gross understatement to say families with children who have disabilities struggle. According to some research, the divorce rate for couples who have children with special needs is nearly 80 percent. As the parents focus so much on their child, it can be nearly impossible to find the time and energy needed for their marriage. Much needed time together can quickly take a back seat to the ongoing, daily responsibilities of caring for someone with special needs.

Jill's House is a Christian nonprofit organization, making respite for these families possible and giving their children an unforgettable overnight experience they can't get anywhere else.

> *"Caring for kids with intellectual disabilities is complex. Whether due to specific behavioral needs, strict medication regimen, or special equipment most people have never seen, parents can't simply call up a babysitter to get a break."* – **Jill's House**

Let's Prep:
Gather art supplies, such as paper, crayons, markers, paints, beads, clay, etc. You can use items you have on hand or purchase new.

Set up a free silent art auction account through 32Auctions at the following website: www.32auctions.com. You can list up to 20 items using their completely free account. You may want to consider collecting your masterpieces over several weeks or invite a friend or family member to join in your efforts. Many hands make light work.

Let's Serve:
Talk with your children about individuals with special needs. Explain how parents of children with special needs have many responsibilities to care for them. Help your children understand what a blessing it would be for these families to have a break from their many responsibilities. Discuss Jill's House and what respite provides to these parents and families. Lastly, enthusiastically explain how this service project will raise funds

to help parents enjoy an afternoon, evening, or weekend to reconnect as a couple or with other family members, while the child has a wonderful experience.

Have your children use the art supplies in whatever manner they choose to create their own masterpieces. Feel free to encourage them to make several works of art. Next, take photos of their artwork and post the photos on the art auction website, including a brief explanation about why your children have created these masterpieces and how the funds will be used to support the work being done through Jill's House. Invite your friends and family to bid on the art. After the auction has ended, donate the funds to donate.jillshouse.org to help sponsor a family for some much-needed respite.

Let's Pray:
Father God, please give our children a heart to love everyone. Bless families raising children with disabilities worldwide. Give them strength, endurance, and a peace that only You can provide. Bless the ministry of Jill's House as they seek to serve families who have children with special needs and share Your love with them. In the name of Jesus, we pray. Amen.

Let's Reflect:

49

Support Military Spouses

> *"May the God of hope fill you with all joy and peace in believing, so that by the power of the Holy Spirit you may abound in hope."* **Romans 15:13**

Let's Talk:

When honoring our military abroad, we can often forget about their families back home anxiously awaiting their return. There is a Christian nonprofit organization called Support Military Spouses. Their mission is "to applaud the brave military wives and husbands who shoulder responsibilities of family, employment, finances, wounded warrior care, and the honoring of fallen heroes." Their goal is to provide appreciation care packages and cards to men, women, and children of deployed military members, letting them know that they are special and valued.

This week, let's talk with our children about ways to encourage and pray for families serving our country from behind the scenes.

Let's Prep:
Gather supplies to make cards, such as card stock, scissors, glue, markers, stickers, etc.

Let's Serve:
As a family, pray for the families waiting for their loved ones to return. Then, discuss ideas on how your family could encourage them. As your children prepare cards and letters, have them include colorful drawings and uplifting Bible verses. For little ones, allow them to have a blast scribbling their heart away. Then, ask them what the scribbles say so you can translate it into English for them.

> *"Caring Cards can touch these individuals more than you know. Lifting them up. Encouraging them. Letting them know they are appreciated. Cards and letters you write will be included with a special Care Package delivered to a military family."* **– Support Military Spouses**

When finished, please mail your cards and drawings to:
Support Military Spouses
1100 Commons Boulevard, Unit 907
Myrtle Beach, SC 29572

If your family decides they want to get more involved, you may choose to sponsor a care package for a spouse or child. Donation information can be found by visiting www.supportmilitaryspouses.org/product/sponsor-care-package.

Let's Pray:

Father God, we ask You to protect and bless our military service members and their families. Give them strength and peace, especially during this difficult time of separation. May they feel loved and cared for through these letters and care packages, and ultimately by You. In the name of Jesus, we pray. Amen.

Let's Reflect:

50

Addressing Bullying

> *"But I say to you who hear, Love your enemies, do good to those who hate you, bless those who curse you, pray for those who abuse you."* **Luke 6:27-28**

Let's Talk:

Bullying is any repetitious harassing behavior towards another individual. Many times, this unwanted and aggressive behavior happens in a school setting. However, bullying can happen anywhere, including after-school programs, scouts, church groups, camps, or anywhere children or teens are gathered.

Bullying in action could be name-calling, teasing, spreading rumors, taking someone's belongings, threatening, or any unwanted action intended to harm another individual. Parents are often unaware of a problem and may not know how to respond.

"Christian parents, quoting Jesus, tell their children to 'turn the other cheek' (Matthew 5:39) when bullied. What's remarkable is that when Jesus was slapped on the face by the guard of the High Priest, He did not turn his face so the guard could slap him again. Instead Jesus responded, 'If I said something wrong, testify as to what is wrong. But if I spoke the truth, why did you strike me?' (John 18:19-23) Jesus not only defended himself with words, He confronted the bully and demanded an answer for his unjust treatment. Since Jesus does not contradict himself, we are given a valuable lesson into what he really meant. He wants his followers to not return an insult for an insult. Jesus, explained C.S. Lewis, does not want his followers to be neither motivated nor consumed by revenge when something wrong like bullying is done to them. But—and this is a key insight into a faith-based response to adolescent bullying—self-defense is not the same as revenge. This fundamental truth is at the heart of Lewis' essay, 'Why I Am Not a Pacifist.' A child can defend himself while at the same time not abuse or demean another person." - **Paul Coughlin, founder of The Protectors**

As parents, one of the best things we can do is have an open line of communication with our children about bullying. We should encourage our children to speak up to us and other trusted adults when they experience or witness bullying. When adults know how to respond and do so quickly, children learn that this behavior is not acceptable and will not be tolerated.

This week, let's talk with our children about bullying and share ways to demonstrate kindness towards their peers.

Let's Prep:

You will need the following:

- » Post-It Notes to make kind and encouraging notes; you may also print some from the following website: www.servingtogether.org/printables

- » Pen or pencil

The day before this service project, place encouraging notes all over your house. You can put notes in a lunchbox, tape notes to your child's door or mirror, or anywhere you think they'll find them.

Let's Serve:

Talk with your children about bullying and how to handle it in a biblical manner. Roleplaying can be a helpful tool. Make sure your children understand that any form of bullying is unacceptable. Encourage them to let you know if this is happening or ever happens to them or others. Urge them to not only stand up for themselves and others being bullied, but to show kindness to those bullying others.

Ask your children how the notes around the house made them feel. As they express their positive feelings, discuss how others would feel receiving the same notes. Talk about places you could leave these notes to encourage others. Allow your children to make some of their own on sticky notes to encourage others. Have your school-age children secretly leave the notes in different places, such as the seat on the bus, a bathroom mirror, or even on a teacher's desk. If your child knows someone who has been picked on in the past, they could leave one on their locker or put one in their seat. Be creative and have fun sharing kindness!

If your children are younger than school-age, they are never too young to show kindness to others. Have your little one help you make a few encouraging notes. With your little one helping, use these encouraging notes to cover your spouse's car window or maybe your neighbor's front door. Talk with your child about how these notes will make the person feel and be excited about it. This is such a fun service project; your little ones will likely ask to do it again.

Let's Pray:
Father God, we pray for children and teens everywhere who are experiencing bullying. We ask You to give them strength and protection. We also pray for those who are being bullies. We pray they would find their self-worth in You and not by making others feel bad. Father God, help our children speak up and stand up for what is right. May they love well, encouraging and showing kindness to others. We ask You to use each of these encouraging notes to give hope and point people to You. In the name of Jesus, we pray. Amen.

Let's Reflect:

51

Empowering Action

> *"Blessed be the God and Father of our Lord Jesus Christ! According to his great mercy, he has caused us to be born again to a living hope through the resurrection of Jesus Christ from the dead,"* **1 Peter 1:3**

Let's Talk:

Various organizations work in many ways to make an impact in impoverished communities worldwide. Empowering Action is a Christ-centered nonprofit organization, seeking to "facilitate long-term development not merely provide short-term aid," in the Dominican Republic, Cuba, and Haiti. They work towards accomplishing this endeavor through their Abundant Life Program.

The Abundant Life Program is a 16-week initiative, training the local church to lead activities with people from their local community and helping them learn simple solutions that will have a big impact on their health and economic empowerment based on the foundation of Christian values.

This week, we will encourage our children to find small ways to make a big difference, while we strive towards teaching our children about poverty worldwide from a Biblical worldview.

Let's Prep:
No preparation is required.

Let's Serve:
Discuss poverty with your children and answer any questions they may have about those living in poverty. I pray God uses this service project to begin developing and growing hearts filled with gratitude and compassion in ourselves and our children.

Talk with your family about small luxuries they enjoy on a daily or weekly basis. It might be a trip to a restaurant your family visits regularly, getting donuts on the weekend or enjoying lattes. No matter how small of a luxury, it quickly adds up to a significant amount of money. Challenge your family to give up a luxury for a certain length of time — maybe a week, two weeks, or even a month. The focus isn't the length of time, but on how the money saved will be used to make an impact for Christ in the lives of impoverished people in developing nations.

After abstaining from the chosen luxury for the designated length of time, visit the following Empowering Action website as a family and donate the money saved: give.empoweringaction. org/abundantlife. Reinforce the importance of the work God is doing in the lives of people through this organization.

Let's Pray:

Father God, we thank You for the blessings You have given us. Help us not take Your blessings for granted. We thank You for the work Empowering Action is doing for Your glory, seeking to live out the Great Commission in areas of great poverty. We thank You for the opportunity to be part of this important work. We ask You to cause our hearts and the hearts of our children to be filled with gratitude and compassion. May we continue to seek out small ways to make a big difference for Your glory. In the name of Jesus, we pray. Amen.

Let's Reflect:

52

Run/Jog/Walk for One

"You shall love the Lord your God with all your heart and with all your soul and with all your might. And these words that I command you today shall be on your heart. You shall teach them diligently to your children, and shall talk of them when you sit in your house, and when you walk by the way, and when you lie down, and when you rise." **Deuteronomy 6:5-7**

Let's Talk:

Does your child have a never-ending supply of energy? Mine certainly do! Joining a local run/walk fundraiser can be a great way to raise money for a cause near to your heart, while also encouraging your family to be active. Every local community has unique Christian organizations hosting run/walk fundraisers. It might be for a pregnancy help center, a church, or a shelter. These events can be a great way for your family to show your support, while also working to instill biblical values in our children's hearts. Plus, you'll have a blast doing it!

This week, we will seek out opportunities to be active as a family and support an important cause in the process. Your family might even enjoy a few walks together in preparation for an upcoming event.

Let's Prep:

If you don't already know of an organization hosting a run/walk, this service project will take a little extra legwork on your part. You can do a quick internet search to find any upcoming run/walk fundraisers in your area. When searching, make sure the event is family-friendly and not just for serious runners.

Depending upon the season and weather, you may need to revisit this project in the spring or fall. Based upon your location, you might not find an organization that you would like to support through a run/walk fundraiser. That's okay! You can plan to do a virtual run. Just pick a Christ-centered organization your family would like to support. Then, have friends and family make a pledge and then complete the run/walk at your family's convenience at a park, around the neighborhood, or even on a treadmill at the gym.

Before presenting this project to your children, make sure you have the details figured out, including the cause, date, requirements, etc.

Let's Serve:

With excitement, talk with your children about the upcoming fun run/walk. Discuss with them the organization you will be supporting and their important mission.

Practice run/walk! You may want to spend a little time before the event going on some walks to prepare. The most common length for this type of event is 5K, which is a little more than 3 miles. Have fun working up your endurance as a family to the 3-mile mark. As you go on walks, don't miss this opportunity to observe and talk about God's creation.

On the big day, remember to have a good time as you serve through this fundraiser. Your family is serving to bring God glory, while being healthy and active!

Let's Pray:
Lord, we thank You for the opportunity to raise support for an organization doing work near and dear to our hearts, while being active as a family. As we prepare for this event and while we are at the event, we ask You to lead our conversations. May these talks be opportunities to share our love for You with our children and others. In the name of Jesus, we pray. Amen.

Let's Reflect:

Made in the USA
Monee, IL
26 December 2019